THE MODERN SINGHS

THE MODERN SINGHS

ABBEY & MONEY SINGH

with Paul Little and Judith Watson

HarperCollins*Publishers*

HarperCollins*Publishers*
Australia • Brazil • Canada • France • Germany • Holland • India
Italy • Japan • Mexico • New Zealand • Poland • Spain • Sweden
Switzerland • United Kingdom • United States of America

First published in 2022
by HarperCollins*Publishers* (New Zealand) Limited
Unit D1, 63 Apollo Drive, Rosedale, Auckland 0632, New Zealand
harpercollins.co.nz

A catalogue record for this book is available from the National Library of New Zealand.

ISBN 978 1 7755 4231 5 (pbk international edition)
ISBN 978 1 7754 9226 9 (ebook)

Cover design by Darren Holt, HarperCollins Design Studio
Front cover image by Pal Productions
Back cover image © Stuff Limited
Photographs in the colour picture section are from the collection of the authors, except as noted: page 5 (bottom) Tony McKay; pages 10–11 Tony McKay; pages 12–13 Pal Productions; page 15 (top) By Makayla.
Typeset in Adobe Garamond Pro by Kirby Jones

Printed and bound by CPI Group (UK) Ltd, Croydon, CR0 4YY

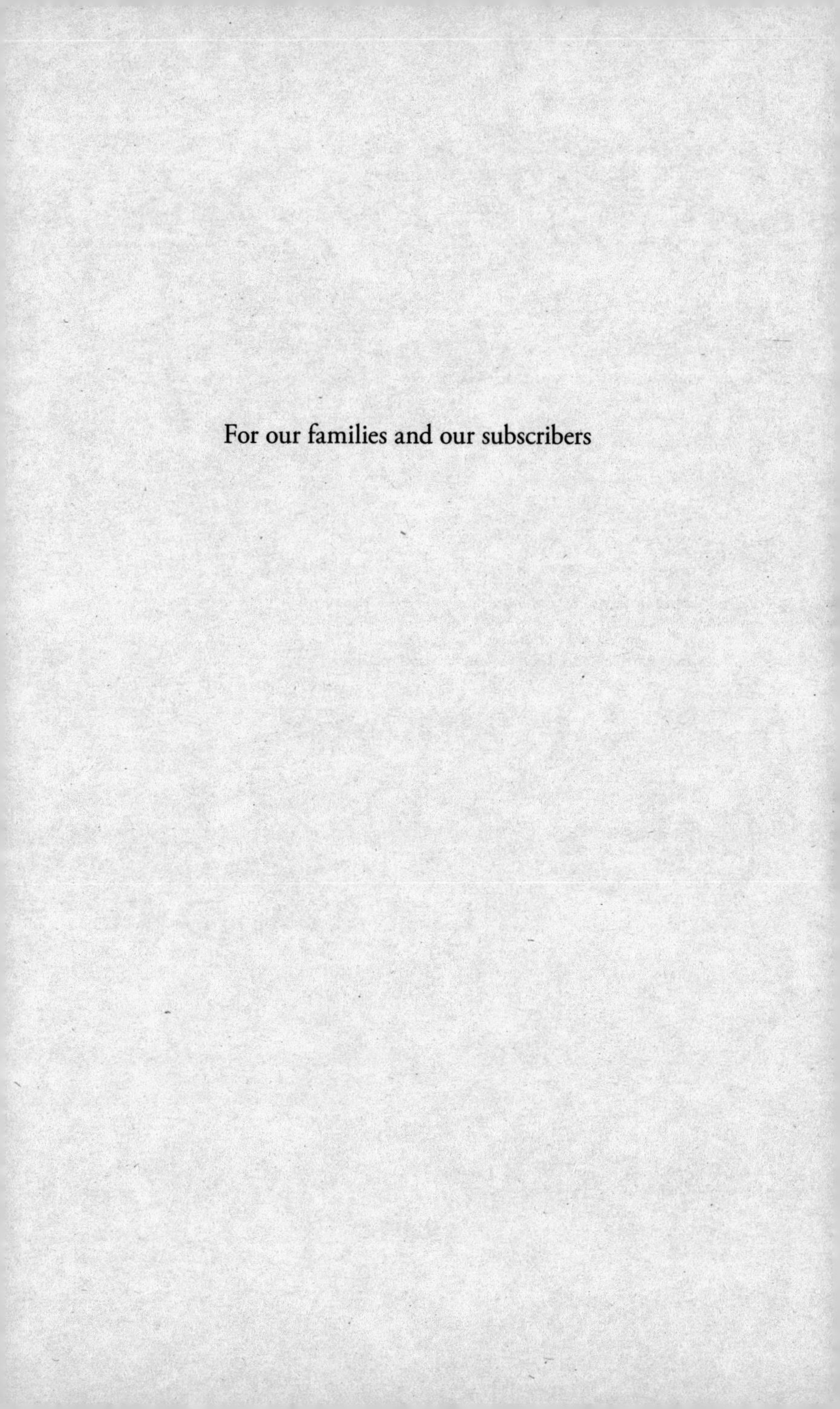

For our families and our subscribers

CONTENTS

invite

Theresa McAleaney requests the honour of
your presence at the marriage of

Abbey Sarah Brown
&
Manminder Singh

On

Thursday the 6th of December
at four o'clock in the afternoon

Markovina Vineyard Estate
84 Old Railway Road, Kumeu
Reception to Follow

ੴ ਸਤਿਗੁਰ ਪ੍ਰਸਾਦਿ ॥

ਕੀਤਾ ਲੋੜੀਐ ਕੰਮੁ ਸੁ ਹਰਿ ਪਹਿ ਆਖੀਐ ਕਾਰਜੁ ਦੇਇ ਸਵਾਰਿ ਸਤਿਗੁਰ ਸਚੁ ਸਾਖੀਐ
ਲੱਖ ਖੁਸ਼ੀਆ ਪਾਤਿਸ਼ਾਹੀਆ ਜੇ ਸਤਿਗੁਰ ਨਦਰਿ ਕਰੇਇ ॥

s/o Sardar Paraminder Singh and Sardarni Amarjit Kaur
Grandson of Late Sardar Inder Singh and Sardarni Manjit Kaur
Request the honour of your presence to grace the auspicious occasion of the marriage ceremony of their son

Manminder Singh

to

Abbey Brown

Daughter of Craig Brown and Theresa Brown

Ceremonies

Anand Karaj

on Friday 14th December 2018 at 11.00am
at Gurdwara Dashmesh Darbar Sahib,
166 Kolmar Road, Papatoetoe, Auckland 2015

Jaggo	**Reception**
12th December, 2018	*15th December - 2018*
at 6.30pm onwards	*at 6.30pm onwards*

Venue

D' Grand Haveli, 736 Great South Rd,
Manukau, Auckland 2104

CHAPTER ONE

The Old Country

MONEY

My parents are both from the Punjab area of northern India but from different backgrounds. My father's name is Parminder (his family nickname is Pindi) and he is from a small village called Bowani. My mother, Amarjeet Kaur, is from the nearby city of Ludhiana. Amar means 'pure'. In New Zealand, everyone calls her Pam; she chose this name as it's an acronym, made up of Parminder, Amarjeet and Money – she said it was a reminder of all three of us. The cool thing is that now, many years later, Mum says the 'A' is also for Arshdeep, my younger brother, and for Abbey, her daughter-in-law, so 'Pam' is a very special name for her.

Mum and Dad had an arranged marriage, which is the traditional way in India. My father is the eldest of five siblings, all of whom had arranged marriages apart from his brother Sukhminder. It was common to get married around seventeen or eighteen, although, in their case, Mum was nineteen and Dad was twenty-five. Many of the traditions are changing these days and, with each new generation, the rules relax and things are more flexible. But, back then, it was imperative that the females in the family get married as soon as possible because the girl's family was required to provide a dowry, which could be expensive and a source of pressure. In an arranged marriage, it is not as much about two people falling in love, as it is about two families joining together. When someone is at the age that they should marry, word travels through the extended family: 'My daughter needs a husband' or 'I am looking for a wife for my son. Can you recommend anyone?' With little access to phones and computers, this was usually done by word of mouth or letters sent by post and, gradually, the message would be passed to more and more people until, eventually, something about a situation or a potential partner would catch the family's attention.

For my parents, there wasn't any dating and no time for romance. Dad was working long hours in a tailor's premises in the town of Doraha, his wages helping to keep the family afloat. A life of socialising was completely out of the question, and girls were not really on his radar. My mother's family were interested in the arrangement because my father's father was well respected in our village. Mum's older sister, who had been like a surrogate mother to her when she was younger, had already married and moved into her husband's family's home, and there were a younger and older brother still at home, but it was time for my mother to get married and start her own life.

My parents had never met before the day they got engaged in the *Gurdwara* (a Sikh temple). Prior to then, they had only seen a photo of one another. This first meeting is important; it is a promise of their bond before God. They married a year after their engagement and had met only two times further during this time: once for a *Lohri* party for a family member, and again at a small engagement party.

I see my parents' relationship as a love story – even more because they had to *learn* to love each other rather than fall in love first. Mum said that when she saw my father she was happy. She said he had a fine beard and nicely tied turban, and she felt very lucky to be arranged to this handsome man. My dad said she was the most beautiful woman he had seen and he was excited to be her husband and spend their lives together.

Some village people are well off and own land that they lease to farmers, but Dad's family was poor. Everyone lived together, my uncles and aunties, my grandmother and grandfather, my great-grandmother. When she got married, Mum moved in and became part of this extended family. She fell pregnant within a few months of being married so it was a lot for her, coming to terms with her first pregnancy, settling in, and because she was now responsible for everything, she took care of the house, did the chores and cooked the meals. It was a real adjustment and she was so busy. She got along really well with my father's parents and quickly became very close to them, which helped her. Everyone was so excited there was going to be a baby.

I was born in Ludhiana Hospital on 13 August 1993. Dad had stayed behind to work when Mum left to give birth, and there was no phone to find out how things were going, but one of our family friends happened to be at the hospital and cycled the 25 kilometres to the village to bring the news that Mum had had a baby boy. Again, things have changed since then, but to have a boy was a big deal at that time as it meant less financial pressure on a family. When I was born they named me Manminder. 'Mani' is the most common nickname to this, but early on, my grandfather started calling me 'Money' and this has been what everybody has called me since.

It is probably difficult for many New Zealanders to imagine the kind of lifestyle I was brought up in and how I spent my first four years before we moved to New Zealand. Even though it was not the most extreme poverty that you find in India, my parents had to work hard to survive. In the city of Ludhiana, Mum's family had gas cylinders and stoves to do their cooking inside the house, but there was none of that in Bowani. To prepare a meal, my mother would first have to make a fire. Every morning, the women went to a farm and collected cowpats, which were brought home and stored to dry out. She would use these to light a fire under a handmade clay stove, out in the garden.

All daily activities were physical tasks. My family couldn't afford to buy milk, but they had a cow at home that Mum milked each morning. The house was just a concrete shell, divided into a few rooms, with no real bathroom or toilet. The windows didn't have glass: the house was boiling hot in summer and freezing cold in winter. There was no plumbing – we didn't have hot water coming out of a tap. Water was pumped from a well and carried home, then a fire was lit to boil it, either for drinking, because it wasn't safe to drink otherwise, or for bathing. Once it was warm, we'd use a scoop to wash ourselves. I remember I couldn't be bothered doing that after a while and just washed myself with cold water. There was no sit-down toilet. You learnt to squat over a hole in the floor. And with no cistern or flush switch, you tipped in another bucket of water to wash everything away.

We didn't use toilet paper because it was too expensive. Once again, the tap and bucket were used.

If you were in a car, this meant you were displaying wealth. In India, you see the poorest and the richest of society, but being wealthy there doesn't mean Lamborghini rich; it means Honda Civic rich. When I was very small, Dad had a motorbike that the three of us would ride on, me standing between Dad's legs, holding onto the handle bars, and Mum on the back. That was our only transportation.

If you have to spend your whole day fetching water and making fire for the most basic of tasks, you will never get ahead because you just don't have the time. That is the economics of it. This was the life I led. I didn't know any other way. Some time later when we took my little brother, who was born in New Zealand, to India, we simply bought him bottled water. Things had changed a lot in just a short time. I think it's important for people to know that the hand-to-mouth existence is only one generation ago. The people who were milking a cow every day in India could well be the same people who now buy their milk from a corner dairy in New Zealand.

Dad's entire immediate family is in New Zealand now, something that took many years and much hard work to achieve. My uncle Sukhminder, called Sukhi, was the first to emigrate. He comes third in the family, after Dad and my aunty, and from an early age, he was motivated to get out of poverty. He didn't just want this for himself; he wanted everyone to benefit, and he was driven to make it happen. Sukhi and my father finished their schooling and were out working by twelve years old. Education was expensive and a luxury many families couldn't afford; not only did you have to pay for it but also you weren't bringing in any money. Dad and my uncle had to grow up quickly and earn, and help find the money to marry off the girls in the family. Girls didn't stay at school long either. They were needed at home to look after the smaller children and do the household chores.

My uncle suggested to my grandfather that everything except the family home should be sold and the money put towards sending him overseas, to start the process of getting the family out of India. At first, everyone was worried by the idea. When you are so poor, selling everything you own is a huge risk. It even meant using the savings my great-grandfather had given to my grandfather, who was to divide it between all the children. A New Zealand woman who owned a tailoring business in Auckland was known to sponsor people from overseas to come and work for her. My father had a friend who had already left under this arrangement, and when he rang them to say she was looking for others, my uncle was one of the lucky ones who got accepted onto the program. He was nervously excited as he set off on his own, with his ticket paid for by the whole family's sacrifices and the equivalent of just NZ$20 in his pocket. On the plane he met others about to undertake the same work in the same factory. None of them could speak English or knew anything about New Zealand, but they did know how to work really hard, and they decided to stick together and share accommodation when they got here, seeing this was normal back home anyway. These people are still in our lives to this day.

My uncle had a lot to learn. Basic things like going to the supermarket was a foreign concept, but from the moment he arrived, he started saving money, not spending anything on himself, and he picked things up quickly. A year later and the company was expanding and needing more staff, so my uncle said, 'My brother is also a tailor,' and that is how my father came to New Zealand. It was his turn to leave behind everything and everyone he knew, including, by this stage, my mother and me. We would wait until the brothers could save up enough money to bring us out next. Although my mum missed my dad, she did not want to leave his elderly parents, who were sick and needed a lot of looking after.

In those early years, life was not so different for Dad in New Zealand. He still worked hard and did long hours, then brought sewing home with him at night, while locals in the area brought more for him to do outside of his work hours, so it seemed to be non-stop. It was only in later years that I really understood what he had done for us, the way he was building a foundation for our family. My uncle Sukhi's approach to bringing the family out was respectful of everyone involved. Along the way there were lawyers' fees and other expenses and my uncle paid them all. Despite taking a loss on his own business because of this financial commitment, his priority was always the family. The rules are different now but, back then, my uncle was first able to bring out one aunty, and once she was sorted, she applied for a visa for her husband and brought him over. And just as my uncle and my dad had been brought out by a business that sponsored them, they could now bring out members of our family to work in their own tailoring business they had set up. After only two years, Dad and Uncle Sukhi were becoming established. They'd got their heads around visas and applications for permanent residency and had managed to save enough money so that by February 1998, they sent for my mother and me to come.

This caused some real heartbreak for my dad's parents, especially my grandfather who was too old to ever make the trip to New Zealand. My younger cousin and I are the only two of his eleven grandchildren he ever met. I don't remember much about him, but I do know of his kindness and that he was a well-known member of the community. He used to be a bus inspector. If he went to the shop and was bringing groceries home and saw a poor or hungry person, he would share his food with them. When my mother and I were leaving, my grandfather was very emotional. He told Mum it was the last time he would see her and that he would not come to the airport because it would make him too sad. He had formed such a special relationship with my mother and me. But, to our surprise, when we arrived at the airport, my grandfather had got there ahead of us, saying he'd changed his mind and had come to say one last goodbye.

I was four years old and didn't have any real idea about where I was going. New Zealand was a long way away – not only was the flight about twenty hours long but the drive just to get to the airport from our village was eight hours. All I knew was that at the end of it, I would see my dad again. This was only the second time my mother had been in a car in her life. The first was when she got married. The plane trip was an incredible experience, but overwhelming. We understood that if we stayed on the plane we would get to our destination and that was all we knew. Everything was foreign. During the stopover in Hong Kong we were too scared to use the chairs and so we sat on the floor in the terminal departure lounge. I left the toys I was given to play with during the trip on the plane in case taking them got us in trouble.

We arrived in Auckland. My parents hadn't seen each other for two years. Sometimes I wonder how Abbey and I would be if we were in a similar situation. Would we be able to stand the separation? It would be so hard, but it would depend on the circumstances. My father and his brother and family knew they had to make these sacrifices or my mother and the others would still be lighting a fire every day to cook a meal. But even though we were now in Auckland, we still had very little. All of us lived in one bedroom, sleeping on mattresses on the floor, with just a curtain to divide our quarters, but we had each other and I remember it as a happy time. I seemed to understand that my friends here had cool new things but we had love and the strength of family. That start in life has made me appreciate everything we have been given.

My dad has so much respect for my mum. He often comments on how none of the progress our family has made would have been possible if she hadn't stayed in India and looked after me and taken care of his parents for as long as she did – but Dad and Uncle Sukhi were so happy to have her with them at last, and her cooking was an added bonus. Dad kept working as hard as ever and so did Mum. This work ethic influenced how I saw my father. It is the same for many Indian parents; their kids might misunderstand and think they are not there for them, but they are working to pay for their schooling and the things they need. My father didn't want me to have to work as hard as him. When I wished to get a paper round, he was discouraging. He just said I should study. And he wasn't an Indian parent with ambitions for me to be a doctor or engineer; he never told me what to be, yet he was conscious that he couldn't study when he was my age but had to go out to work so he didn't want me to waste the opportunities. My uncle was the same – he is very smart and always said he wished he could have studied law.

My father and his brother were on a two-year contract when they arrived, which gave them a weekly income. There were no restrictions on how much they could work and sometimes they worked six or even seven days a week. They were very proud of the fact that they never said no to a shift. In that time, they didn't go out, my uncle didn't date girls, he was so focused on earning enough money. It's even more amazing when you think my uncle was just twenty-three when he came here. And together, he and Dad spent almost nothing and saved everything they could. They gave up their lives to get their family here. They didn't try to make friends, they just had each other. Once they had fulfilled their obligation to the Auckland business, they started a company called Sagu Fashions, and they worked harder than ever. By this time, we were living in a rented house with all the sewing machines they needed in the double garage. They would be at work when I went to school in the morning, still at it when I got back, and they'd keep working into the night.

ABBEY

My mum, Theresa, and my dad, Craig, started dating when they were very young. They met while out having drinks with work mates in their small hometown in Scotland. My dad noticed my mother straightaway and approached her, and she says they hit it off immediately. I think they were actually pretty happy when she got pregnant, and in those days they were really good together. They decided to get married. Mum was nineteen when they had their first child (my older sister, Nicole), then two years later my brother, Jack, was born and I came along four years after, on 22 June 1996, christened Abbey Sarah Brown. By the time Mum was twenty-five, she had three kids under six. When I think about how much of a handful it is with just a busy one-year-old, what my mother managed seems almost impossible. When I ask her about it now, she says she loved those years and looks back on them fondly, although if she were to change anything it would have been to not stress so much. She said she couldn't have done any of it without her parents, who looked after us a lot – their place was literally our second home.

Unfortunately, Mum and Dad didn't have the most stable of relationships, which added to the normal pressures of being young parents. There was not much money. We lived in a two-bedroom apartment in a very small complex in Bellshill, North Lanarkshire; my parents in one room and the three of us children in the other. Theirs was an on-again/off-again relationship. Dad left Mum for the first time when I was six weeks old, again when I was about two, and so the pattern continued. Since before I was born, he'd been a forklift operator for a large supermarket company. It suited him. He was comfortable, he had friends there and he knew the job well enough, he probably didn't see the point in looking for other work.

But my parents had very different personalities. Dad was happy just to take life as it came, while Mum wanted to try and improve things for herself and for us. I've decided I am a mix of both of them. When they were going through all of this, my mother was studying to be a midwife and holding down a 9-to-5 office job. She worked so hard: a busy job, three kids and a full-time course of study. My grandmother was Mum's rock, and ours, and she helped out with a lot of childcare. She and Grandpa lived a couple minutes' drive away and I was there every chance I got. She was, and is to this day, my everything. Her name is Josephine; she's this little, sweet old lady – but fiery! She was always the best company, and an amazing cook. She'd make us a big plate of pancakes with syrup every morning, she'd cook family roast dinners with apple pie for dessert on the weekends. When we walked around the town together, she was so active and fit, she could walk faster than me. I remember she loved to record my favourite movies or TV shows on VHS so that when we went over there, we could sit together on the couch and watch them. Granny is just the most amazing person. She's still alive and well, living in Bellshill, where everybody knows her.

Mum's commitment to her study paid off and she qualified as a midwife – but that didn't mean the hard work came to an end. She was busier than ever, in some very stressful situations, doing twelve-hour shifts at the local hospital. Meanwhile, Dad came and went, but it still felt like we saw a lot of him because during the periods when my parents weren't together, he would move back in with his mother, who lived only a short drive away. One day, when I was still young, we were due to visit my grandparents on dad's side for dinner but got a call during the day to tell us that my grandfather had died suddenly. My dad was very close to his father and, looking back on this, we think he never really recovered from the shock, and perhaps it wasn't handled in the way traumatic events are these days, with grief counselling available and so on. His father's death also made Dad very protective of his mum, making sure she had everything she needed and, subconsciously, worrying that something might happen to her, so he has never liked to be too far away. This is maybe another reason why it didn't work out when he followed us to New Zealand later on.

The whole back and forth of whether Dad was with us or not occurred so often – it made things really unsettling for us kids. We never knew what was going on. Oh, great, Mum and Dad are together. Now things will be okay. Oh, no, they're not. It was so stressful keeping up with it all. More than once I remember coming home from school and his suitcases were at the door. *No, not again*. That must have happened eight or nine times. If we hadn't loved our dad so much, this pattern of behaviour might have been easier to handle, but he was such fun and so loving that we were excited every time he came back and it looked like we would be a family once more. Then my heart would break and I would cry myself to sleep as he left. Then a couple of months later he would be back. It was killing us.

I believe that witnessing what my parents went through to try and make it work has had a real impact on what I want out of relationships and it set my expectations as to what I looked for in a man. I value trust, communication and honesty over anything else in a relationship – and I found all of that in Money, thankfully. But it did make me afraid that someone would leave me one day, and I've had to work very hard on getting rid of feelings of mistrust and doubt, as I know they're not healthy to carry around.

CHAPTER TWO

New New Zealander

MONEY

There was no official support for us when we arrived – no orientation program or material to tell us what we needed to know about life in New Zealand, like there is now. Neither my dad nor my uncle had had time to do anything to get ready for us. Their life was solely about work. Dad was focused on the fact he would be seeing us, but he didn't think, *My son will be here soon, I had better organise a doctor and school and everything else he will need.* Fortunately, next door to where my father and uncle were living was a lovely woman whose children had left home by then and she took an interest in us. She helped settle us in and showed my mum where to buy things and everything that was part of day-to-day living – but compared to what is now available for migrants to this country, it was very much about fending for ourselves and working it out.

There were a few hiccups and learning curves. I remember one time when I was small, Mum went to the supermarket and left me at home because I didn't want to go. In India it was usual to be home alone or watched over by other members of the family. 'All right, just stay here and watch *Teletubbies* till I get back,' said Mum. She didn't know there was a minimum age for leaving kids home alone. When *Teletubbies* finished I decided the logical thing was to go and find her. I knew where the supermarket was, and I also remembered that if I shut the door behind me it would lock, so I cleverly placed a book in the doorway to hold it open, just in case. I managed to get there by myself but, in the meantime, Mum had used a different route to come back home. When she arrived into an empty house, she naturally freaked out. She called the police as well as my father. Dad was crying, saying, 'I can't believe it. You have only just come to New Zealand and now we have lost our son.' But finally a connection was made between a lost child at the supermarket and a woman whose child was missing, and the police took me home. They told my parents if something like this happened again, their son would be taken away from them. This was a major wake-up call for

Mum that we were clearly living in a very different world from the one we had left.

Our kind neighbour came with us to help enrol me at Target Road Primary School. Back in India I had been to kindergarten for just a month, where we sat three to a desk in long rows. All that I remember about the place was one day getting hit with a ruler. There was a monkey playing outside the classroom window and I kept watching it instead of paying attention, and I got hit for being distracted. Not long after I started at Target Road, I was talking to a friend when the teacher came up to us. I automatically put my hand out to be hit because I thought I was in trouble.

Mum started sewing at a curtain factory. Dad went to work every morning and she'd go to work in the evenings. By now we had other relatives and family friends living with us so there was always someone around to look after me. Then Mum found work during the day as well. When I started school, Mum didn't tell me but for two weeks she followed me to school and sat outside to keep an eye on me, she was so worried about how I would settle in and how they would treat me because I wore a turban. Nowadays, there is an extensive Indian community where we live, but back then someone like me was pretty unusual.

'Every time I looked in the classroom, it broke my heart,' she told me later, 'because all the kids would be in one corner and you would be on your own in another.' This was true, the other kids did reject me and I didn't know how to interact, especially as I spoke almost no English. On my first day, the teacher said something to me, and I answered her in Punjabi, saying, 'I want to go home.' Mum said that I had to keep going to school and not give up – just like my parents had shown me. I picked up the language quickly, being around a lot of English-speaking kids, and we were all at the same age to learn our ABCs and so on. For my parents it was different. My uncle, having arrived first, knew he could only rely on himself and must learn English quickly and he was the most fluent speaker in the family. He did all the talking to clients. Dad was more involved in the technical side of the business and didn't need to have conversations with people, so his English fell behind. And at Mum's work, she didn't have to communicate much, while at home we only spoke Punjabi.

A real point of difference at school was to do with my hair. Following Punjabi tradition, my hair had never been cut, and I wore a *patka*, a child's turban. At night, Mum washed my hair, and in the morning she braided it and wrapped it around my head. Then a white square of material was placed on top, and then the *patka*. I wore this each day for my first year at school. A lot of people called it my pompom, which sounds racist, but they didn't know the proper name for it and didn't realise using that terminology would be offensive. And they couldn't deal with my name, Manminder, making fun of it and calling me Mandarin, instead. So I soon became Money at school, as well as with my family.

I often came home and cried because no one wanted to be my friend. I still couldn't speak much English. I felt so different from everyone else and they didn't know anything about what it meant to be Sikh, or understand why my hair was long. It was very hard making friends. Sometimes boys pulled off my turban or pushed me into the girls' toilets, saying I belonged there because I had long hair. By then my hair was down to my lower back. The principal was very kind and would try to wrap my hair back up, and she learnt how to tie the turban and put that back on. At home I would beg my parents to let me have my hair short so I could be like the other kids. If I had stayed in India, I might never have had it cut; it is partly a reflection on how strong the values of our culture are held. My dad always wore a turban in India but he cut his hair when he came to New Zealand. This was a huge religious sacrifice to make, but when you are in another culture, sometimes it pays to be flexible. It wasn't an easy decision for them to let me, either, but they also understood it would make it easier to fit in and therefore get ahead. I know if my father hadn't cut his, they would have insisted I keep my hair long, so I am glad they had already made that compromise.

'Oh, so pretty,' said the barber when he uncovered the *patka* and my hair tumbled down. He put purple clips over my head. I was regarded as pretty when I was little, and a lot of people thought I was a girl, but on this day, Mum still thought I was getting a regular haircut; I knew differently.

'Mum, this isn't a boy cut,' I said in Punjabi. I'd seen enough movies and TV shows by then to know. 'He thinks I'm a girl. This is what a girl would get.'

'You don't know anything about haircuts. Be quiet and sit still,' said Mum. That's another thing about being in a different country, you assume the people there know more than you.

When the barber took the clips out and admired his work, he said, 'There. It looks so nice, doesn't it?'

'You know I'm a boy, don't you?' I asked.

He apologised and quickly did it again and I got a Leonardo di Caprio-style cut with a centre part. I felt so good. There was a girl who lived near us who was my friend, and when we got home I rushed to show her my new hair. 'You look so different and cool,' she said.

I was relieved. I wasn't excited because it was a way of getting out of my culture, I was excited to be able to walk around without getting stared at. Over time, I made more friends and became more confident. I was a six-year-old social butterfly.

A haircut is cheap, but there were many things that were part of normal life in New Zealand that we couldn't afford. When I was in primary school, the first computer that came into our house was from the inorganic rubbish collection. It was one of the iMac versions that were produced in bright green or purple. At first, after I'd carried it all the way home, I couldn't get it going. Then I worked out it needed a power cable and we bought one from The Warehouse. When I finally managed to turn it on, there was a message saying it had twenty-eight days left to go. I made the most of it, waking up every morning so keen to turn it on and play. It had just one game. There was no internet connection or anything, I was simply exploring what a computer was and what it could do, going through the settings and finding out random things about it.

Our family loved the inorganics because we found so much stuff, but I still used to feel disappointed about the many things we couldn't have because we didn't have the money.

'Be patient,' Mum said. 'The time will come one day. God has everything planned.'

In my mind, the inorganic rubbish collection was part of God's plan, and for the week or so it occurred each year, it became a family project. My aunty would drop my cousin and me off to walk through the streets and see what we could find. Apart from the computer, which was the very best thing, I found lots of other useful things my parents would never have been able to afford. I got a scooter and a bike, and a pair of rollerblades and taught myself how to skate. Naturally, I hurt myself doing that – and that was a big deal. For the nine years before my little brother was born, I was the very precious only child, and whenever I hurt myself everyone panicked. One day I was going down a steep driveway in our street on the rollerblades, I ended up going faster and faster until I hit a rock and went flying. My parents came rushing to where I was, but before she did anything else, my mum slapped me. 'I told you not to do anything stupid. Now look at you,' she growled.

My dad wasn't far behind. He slapped me too and told me off for being careless. My friend who was with me was wondering what the hell was going on, but I understood. They were taking out their frustration because I had ignored them and taken a risk. Yet, children have to do things on their own in order to learn. They have to make mistakes and find things out for themselves. Despite the smacks and the yelling – or maybe because of them – I knew my parents cared for me and I did feel protected.

I also got hit by both my parents on another occasion when I'd stolen a Pokémon card from a neighbour's place.

I was going through a stage where I didn't understand why I couldn't have all the things I wanted, so if I saw something, I took it. This time they didn't just get mad at me, they were sad. It went against everything we stood for. 'We came to this country to make our lives better,' yelled my mother. 'You are not stealing. If you can't buy it, you are not stealing.'

I felt different from other kids in countless ways. I was self-conscious about everything, even the lunch I brought to school. Other kids had muesli bars and yoghurt and apples. I had Indian food every day – *roti* (pan-fried flat bread) and curries such as *daal* (lentils), *chole* (chickpea) or *saag* (spiced spinach) – all of which have a strong aroma, and even though I don't remember getting teased about it, I didn't want to open up the container in front of others because I was worried it might smell funny. I used to find a quiet corner and eat my lunch on my own.

No one went out of their way to teach me English at primary school. I learnt by full immersion, and by being confident enough to talk to my teachers and classmates. It took me a while to make friends and I spent a lot of time alone, but I always enjoyed my own company. Learning English properly took ages. When my mother and I arrived in New Zealand, we only went to places where Punjabi was spoken. Later, after more of my relations came out from India, I became the family's expert in English. My aunties and uncles were so busy working they didn't stop for language lessons and would ask me to translate anything they couldn't understand. Because I had to work out so many things for myself, I couldn't afford to be shy. I gradually began to fit in to this new culture and country. But I never spoke English with my parents, and we still speak Punjabi to each other.

I have a real regret from this time: it is hurtful to admit (although maybe it's something many immigrant children feel) that when you are an outsider you don't want people to see your parents because you think they will judge you and think less of you. You want to be seen as belonging to your new country, not your old one. My parents were always working so hard, they didn't have time to attend many school events, but one time, Mum had a day off and came to watch the cross-country race. She even brought me McDonald's as a treat. As soon as I saw her there I told her to go. I didn't want her to stay and watch. She left, and I regret that incident so much.

Another time, the school was holding a disco and I asked a girl to be my partner. She said yes, which made my stomach do flips – I was starting to fit in and be normal. The next day I was there when her father dropped her off at school and I heard their conversation.

'Dad, that is the boy I'm going to the disco with.'

'You are not going with an Indian boy,' I heard him reply.

It was such a shock. She came to me and said: 'I'm so sorry. My dad says we can't go together.'

Until then I really thought I was the same as everyone else and that the only difference had been my turban. I didn't realise my race made me stand apart. I didn't fully understand a lot of what would be called racism; I just brushed off most of it as people joking or playing tricks on me. But there were things like that disco incident that reminded me I wasn't the same as others.

When I went to other kids' houses, I always wanted to try their food, and yet I didn't understand why they'd be interested to come to mine and have Indian food. And I was very sensitive to smell – not just my lunchbox. I used to worry about what kids would think when they came, in case the house smelt of curry; I brushed my teeth a lot, and when I was a bit older took lots of showers and used Lynx Africa to hide any smell that was 'foreign'. Yet, I never looked at my friends' lives and wished mine was like theirs. Also my parents were loosening up about some things that might have made life with friends difficult, which helped me. For instance, in the strict Sikh religion, you don't eat any meat, but my parents were relaxed about this. We never ate beef at home, but Mum would cook chicken sometimes, and when I was at other houses, I was allowed to try food like sausages and pasta. So I didn't end up having too many questions or doubts about my culture because I was learning to stretch some boundaries as well.

My parents stayed largely within their culture. There were a lot of other immigrant families living around us – it was like a little India, so they didn't have to speak English or try to learn the new ways. I was the one who was learning the language and picking up on New Zealand customs. They encouraged this because they knew it was the way for me to survive, whereas they didn't have to. Traditionally, the generation that enables a migration to happen stays in their own culture while their kids explore the new culture. I was enjoying this new life, while Mum and Dad were still living their old village life with a few adjustments – like plumbing.

Right from the start, I knew to be careful about how much I told Mum and Dad about this Kiwi lifestyle. All I wanted to do was go to the park, build treehouses and do kid things. I wanted to ride my scooter and go rollerblading. I never did anything my parents would have completely disapproved of, but that is because I found a circle of friends who were not troublemakers. I was lucky. On the other hand, I never came home and did my homework. After school, I'd head out to the park until eight or nine o'clock at night, only returning when the streetlights came on. My parents were busy and didn't notice, although sometimes my mum would come to the park, screaming, 'Get home, Money, dinner is ready.' But my parents didn't know – because they had no way of knowing and I didn't tell them – that I was supposed to be doing homework. They thought whatever I did was the New Zealand way.

Looking back, I can see I was quite spoilt. I was surrounded and supported by so much love, especially from my mother. The next child to come into our family was my uncle's son, Parmjot. I loved babies, but Punjabi culture meant the baby was always with my aunty's side of the family, not ours. I complained that we didn't see the baby more, but Mum just said, 'That is how it is.' Then in 2002, I finally got my own little brother. I had been asking for one for a long time. Mum gave birth to a boy, Arshdeep, who we call Ash. I was super excited, and from the start I treated Ash like I was his father, and to this day we have that bond. I have always looked after him.

From age four until I was twelve years old, this was me. I was trying to understand another country, its rules, its customs, its people. I was also getting to know myself and how I should fit in. It was a daily balancing act; I was learning what did and didn't make me a new New Zealander but I was also trying to stay true to my family and our Punjabi way of life. It was a constant juggle, every day.

ABBEY

Scotland means the world to me and I am proud to say that is where I am from. I lived there until my last year of primary school. The weather is known to be pretty miserable but I always remember the most amazing winters – we'd run and play in the snow and make snowmen and angels. I have brilliant memories from those times. Mine was a busy childhood and we worked hard, especially with Mum being so busy, so I remember a lot of chores such as ironing clothes or doing the dishes. My mum says that when we were young, my brother and I were inseparable, always together playing games, and my older sister was like our second mother, making sure we were okay. My sister was usually the one to comfort me when I cried. I tried to not let my mum see me upset as I knew she was going through a lot herself. It is interesting that this is a strong memory from those years, as it came back up when I was older and finally reached out to her.

We moved to New Zealand when I was eleven. It was 2007. I was older than Money had been when he migrated, and my family's move was under quite different circumstances. Mum had already been out to New Zealand on holiday to visit her sister who lived here with her Scottish husband and their three children, and she had fallen in love with the place. It was safe and sunny and she could see what a comfortable life we could have growing up here.

'We are going to live in New Zealand for a year,' Mum announced when she got home from this trip – but I think she had already decided we were actually moving here permanently. Dad knew about the move and signed consent forms to allow her to take us away. I'm sure he probably wasn't all that happy about it but he must have realised it was inevitable and that everybody needed a fresh start. I think I was too young to fully understand I wouldn't be able to see my granny whenever I wanted or my friends just around the corner. I just was told it was a sunny country where I could go to the beach often, and our two cats, Harry and Hermione (we are massive *Harry Potter* fans), were to be looked after by my granny. It was only after I had been in New Zealand for a while that it really hit me: I didn't have my dad or my grandmother or anything that was familiar around me. Life became harder before it got easier.

I know that my grandmother was understandably devastated when Mum told her the plan, especially considering she already had one daughter living so far away in New Zealand, but Granny is so kind-hearted and full of wisdom, she'd have known this was for the best and that we needed to go. Granny is always helping other people. She would give her last penny to you if you needed it. She is like a celebrity in her town; everyone loves her. If I am walking down the street with her, wherever we go people call out, 'Hello, Josephine. How are you today, love?' She is the best thing ever. As well, she was such a caring wife to our grandpa, and she knew she had to be there for him.

Mum was now a trained midwife, so we did not have to wait to be sponsored before we could move because it was one of the careers on the skills shortage list for migrants. Mum secured a midwifery position immediately at a hospital in Auckland. Only later did I get that when we arrived, Mum, my sister, my brother and I were granted permanent residency – another indication that Mum was planning for us to stay more than a year. By the time I realised we were staying here for good, I had grown used to it and had made friends. At that age, so long as your home life is secure and isn't a threat, then it is easier to go along with whatever the adults in your life are deciding for you.

Even though I spoke English, there were still a lot of differences between Scotland and New Zealand to deal with and adjustments to make. It wasn't as bad for me as it was for Money. The equivalent would be if I were to move to India at age eleven – I can't imagine how hard that'd be. I am so proud of Money for how he handled the transition to the other side of the world. But there were still a lot of challenges to face as a new New Zealander. My accent for one. People were constantly asking me to repeat words that didn't sound right to them, although they sounded just fine to me. I wasn't an outgoing, confident girl until I knew what was what, and so some of those first months, especially at school, were terrifying. Everyone seemed to talk so fast and I was finding it hard to keep up, despite my being the 'different' one that 'spoke funny'. I remember on one of my first days at school, some classmate remarked that they liked my pants. I could feel my face go bright red and I nearly ran and hid in the toilets – in Scotland, they would be referring to my underwear, but here it simply meant the jeans I was wearing. It is often the small things that can trip you up. But what people really noticed and wouldn't stop commenting on was my complexion, which is pale by any standards, but is even paler than most. They used to make fun of me at school, calling me Casper the Ghost. I often went home crying because of the teasing.

I missed my friends at home, but there were many things to like about being here. I loved the warm climate and the beaches, compared to rainy, cold Scotland. I feel like I quite quickly adjusted. And possibly as a way of surviving, I stopped missing home and told myself this is how it is now. My friends in Scotland sent me letters and gifts sometimes, which meant so much to me – I definitely still miss some of these first friends – but I spent all of my energy trying to fit in. Feeling like I wasn't fitting in or didn't belong was way worse for me than any teasing. It made me become quite a people-pleaser, which I would say I still am in danger of being to this day and is something I work on.

My brother was fifteen and my sister seventeen when we emigrated, so they found it much harder than I did. They were taken away from their friends and social lives that were already well established, but then after we'd been here a year or so, my brother didn't want to go back. He made good friends, and enjoying the lifestyle in New Zealand. He started dating a girl when he was seventeen or eighteen – and they are still together and now married. Right now he is actually living back in the UK, but that is because there are more opportunities for his work in TV and as a film editor. My sister also went back to the UK for a while, but she has since moved back here and works in education. She loves her job and it is so awesome having her back close to us, and Noah.

With Mum and Dad's on-again/off-again relationship, my father came to New Zealand a few times, then he went back, then he came over again. The first time he arrived, it was for a few weeks around the time of my sister's eighteenth birthday. He came with Granny, which was just the most special reunion and we had a brilliant time showing her all around Auckland and Waiheke Island, but Dad didn't have a visa so we knew it was a visit and he wouldn't stay long. Then he came out twice more to try to make it work, but it didn't. Either he couldn't settle or he was missing Scotland or there wasn't enough to keep him here. By then, I was around thirteen and I could see that my parents were both trying, for sure, but I don't think they were meant to be together. I was definitely sceptical and didn't want to get my hopes up that we would be a family again. I remember on one of the visits, Dad's brother had just passed away in Scotland, but his ticket was already booked to come before this happened, so he wasn't really in the mindset to put in the energy and effort required. By the third time, we had all pretty much had enough; it was just too hard on everyone. We tried our best, but in the end it wasn't meant to be and, actually, the way it worked out was for the best. Also my father was concerned about his own mother and it affected where he thought he should be living.

When he was heading back to Scotland for what would be the last time, none of the family even went to the airport to see him off. They were done with the back and forth. I was the only one who wanted to say goodbye properly. I was fifteen. I was finding the whole thing really difficult, as was Dad, and I remember waiting with him in the driveway for the taxi to come and pick him up. 'Why are you upset?'

I asked him. 'I'll see you again soon.' I truly believed this, because he always came back. But he didn't after that. And those words came back to haunt me.

Then we had a falling out. He kept asking me to come for a visit and I didn't want to – I had all sorts of teenage things of my own going on, like friends and school. My mum still went back to see family every couple of years but I never wanted to go with her. It was too hard for me to keep saying goodbye again and again. I think that killed my dad a bit. I regret it now.

When no one knows where they stand in a family situation like this, it is very difficult to manage, mentally and emotionally. We were always so happy when my father was coming out, and we missed him when he wasn't here, but I'm not sure he really got how draining it was for us. We were becoming involved in our own stuff. We'd get used to him not being around and then we'd hear he was coming again. I'd have my hopes built up then knocked back down. My mum tried to make it work, and she wanted us kids to have our father around – we really loved him. He was her first love and she hadn't dated anyone throughout all of this, not until we were all grown up, long after their relationship had ended and they divorced.

Back then, I could see that my parents had different aims and goals in life. Mum wanted to better herself and provide for us, whereas Dad was complacent and happy with his lot. After one of the times they broke up, Mum bought a house a street away from where we had been living in a rental. It was such a secure feeling to have our own home. She worked constantly to give us the things she didn't have when she was our age, and I will always admire her for how hard she tried and how she brought us up on her own. Mum wanted to ensure that our needs were met, if she could, so if we wanted to do something and the money wasn't there, such as dance classes or piano lessons, she just worked harder to pay for them.

I realise that although it is the ideal to have two loving parents, it is more ideal to have a stable upbringing, and that is what my mum provided. I wouldn't wish it on anyone to see your parents continuously fighting and arguing. Yet, as well as appreciating that they gave it everything to make it work, it has done a lot for my own strength of character. It's made me evaluate the sort of life I want and what sort of partner I need. I used to think I was the only one going through this when I was young, but there are plenty of dysfunctional families, and it is about finding support and love within that, and then, as an adult, trying to break the cycle. Being a parent myself has made me understand a whole lot more and even why Mum was so angry with Dad. I feel very lucky not to have gone through the things she did. She comes from a strong Roman Catholic background, and it can't have been easy getting pregnant so young and facing the pressures of that. I'm really grateful that they had the three of us, because we have each other to fall back on and we're still close. There's a lot of strength needed to leave one home and begin again in another; it toughens you up.

CHAPTER THREE

Fitting In

MONEY

When I was twelve, Mum decided I would go back to India for a year. It was a confusing time because I didn't want to go, but by the end of that year, I didn't want to come back to New Zealand. One of the reasons for my mother's decision was because of an older teenager who'd started hanging around my circle of friends and he was a bad influence, introducing us to things like cigarettes. I wasn't interested in smoking particularly, but I knew my parents would disapprove, and at that age when your parents have that attitude to something, you want to break the rules because it is exciting to be rebellious. And there was pressure from friends.

The move from primary to intermediate school had been a big transition, with me trying to sort friends, attitudes and social life, and all those questions like, *Am I cool enough? What do I need to do to fit in?* My parents never went to school, so they didn't understand these things, but my mother obviously had an idea there was something going on. She and my dad were putting in so many hours at work they didn't have time to watch me or monitor my behaviour. Her solution was to send me to India to live with her older sister for a year. Fortunately, my aunty is great. It was a huge responsibility for her, but she treated me like one of her own; her three children were older and as well as being company for me, she'd have time to keep an eye on me. She made sure I was well fed and looked after, and I appreciated so much everything she did for me.

When I had first come to New Zealand, I never felt like an outsider – at least, not until I started school, when I was definitely one. But I felt like one again when I returned to India – the way I spoke, my understanding of people, even my New Zealand Punjabi culture was different from Indian Punjabi culture. The restrictions on what you could and couldn't do, rules about what males and females were allowed, what was considered appropriate or not – everything was different. And even though I spoke Punjabi, everyone noticed and commented on my accent. I would say words like a foreigner and they would mock me for this. Seeing India again and learning about it made me appreciate and value the rules my parents lived by. If my mum had not sent me to India, I have no idea what I might have got into or who I might have become.

I really enjoyed getting to know my mother's side of the family. Because it was my father's brother who came to New Zealand and brought the family out, I knew those relatives much better than Mum's. This is one of the disadvantages to migrant life – you lose contact and connections with the people you'd be close to otherwise. And my mother's relatives are very different to Dad's. They are less serious, they don't take things to heart and I found I could joke around with them. Everyone always seemed to be in a good mood. Another difference was that their family was relatively well off – my uncle was in the construction business, my aunt didn't go out to work and my cousins were students. Nowadays, I should say, there is lots more laughing in Dad's family, too. I guess, back then, because of the pressure and stress of getting established in New Zealand and having to work all hours, there weren't so many fun times. It's different now. They are much more relaxed and are able to enjoy themselves a lot more.

Mum came with me and stayed a few weeks in Ludhiana to help me settle in. It was important to her that my education didn't suffer and there was enough money saved up to attend a good school, but it took us quite a while to find one. We went around so many, but a number of them turned me down because I couldn't read or write Punjabi. They said I would cause issues and make things complicated. Day after day we went out looking and were rejected. We started near my aunt's home but kept having to look further and further away. Eventually, I was enrolled at one called Guru Ram Dass Academy (GRD), named after one of the 10 Sikh gurus, although there is no special connection between him and the school. GRD was a long way from my aunt's house, and to me it was like one of those high schools in an American movie. It was huge, with many students and amazing facilities, especially for sports like swimming and basketball, and cricket, of course.

Starting school and settling in was hard. Once again I was bullied for being different. And when I wasn't being bullied, I was ignored and had no one to talk to. I couldn't see any difference between me and everyone else, but they'd all call me a name it took me a while to understand: 'Hey, NRI? Where are you from, NRI?' I found out this meant 'non-residential Indian'. It's changed now, but back then, there weren't many who would leave to go and live overseas, so someone like me was unusual, and there was this belief that those who emigrated might think they were better than everyone else. Being NRI meant I was no longer seen as a true Indian because we were required to give up our passports in order to obtain permanent residency in New Zealand – that was the rule then. So when you come back to India after that, you have to apply for a visa. So even though I had been born in India, now I was seen as a foreigner. And when we first came to New Zealand, I was seen as a foreigner. In India, however, it was more to do with loyalty. People in our situation were criticised for having given up part of their Indian identity, even though it had been done to get something that they themselves wanted – a better life.

No one wanted to be my friend at school in the early days. I tried to mind my own business. One day, a boy pushed me into a wall and punched me for no reason. I couldn't understand why this was happening. The teacher saw me crying. She called me up to the front of the class and told the other students to start talking to me, which was embarrassing, but it worked. I slowly began to make some good friends. One of them lived about thirty minutes from my aunt's place, and one day we were going to the movies and he planned to pick me up on his moped, but my aunt said I wasn't allowed. 'You're not going with anyone,' she told me. 'You don't know what they want from you. Someone could try to kidnap you.' She was really worried about me. It was a big responsibility for her to have me there, so far away from my home and my parents. 'Unless your mother says you can, I won't let you. We can't afford to have anything happen to you.'

I don't think there was anything especially risky about where I was, I just think my aunt was being super cautious. In New Zealand, I guess we took our safety for granted. I cried and made a fuss because I couldn't see her point of view. 'I just want to watch a movie with my friend.'

'You must always think the worst, Money. You have to be prepared for bad things to happen.'

Still, her family made sure I got the most out of my time with them and experienced many aspects of the culture. Every month it seemed someone was getting married, so I went to lots of weddings and other family gatherings. With Mum and Dad, going on a trip might mean driving just a couple of hours south to meet relatives in Hamilton. My aunt and uncle drove six hours one time so I could visit the snow, which I had never seen before, and they hired a bus and a whole lot of us went to Kullu Manali, about nine hours away, in the northern Himachal Pradesh state. It's breathtaking, with its scenery and nature in this amazing national park. Another time we went on a temple tour including a visit to one of the holiest places to Sikhs, the Golden Temple in Amritsar, which was so incredible – and it would be whether you are Sikh or not. Hundreds of thousands of people visit every year. I had heard of the Golden Temple but didn't know much apart from the fact the dome is made from real gold. It looks like it is floating on water, which is just an optical illusion; it's surrounded by a man-made lake. The temple has four doors, to show openness and acceptance. It was an eye-opener for me to see so many there who have devoted their lives to Sikhism, and it made me think a lot, because I was born into that religion and have left so much of it behind. I liked that for a tourist destination, it's just a voluntary donation to enter, and anyone is welcome to visit and learn about the Sikh culture. I felt very humbled and moved by the whole experience.

But a really unsettling thing you see there – as you see almost everywhere in India – is such huge amounts of poverty. Poor people congregate to beg from the rich tourists, both local and foreign. For some, it is just a scam, but you always know that if you give to one person, soon you will be surrounded by a whole crowd of others.

In my mind, I thought I was being sent to India just to become better at speaking and understanding Punjabi, but of course, there was a whole education to be had. Every day, there was so much to adjust to. For instance, in New Zealand, when you catch a bus, you walk to the closest bus stop. In India, the bus stops wherever you are. I had to catch one at 7.30 every morning for school and my cautious aunty would wait with me until it came. Each day before class there was an assembly and we sang the national anthem. I had no idea how to sing it as I'd never heard it before, and even after a year, I never learnt it properly. Because there are so many Punjabi people in Ludhiana, the language gets taught alongside Hindi and English, so as you go through school you could end up knowing three languages. In New Zealand, I would have been learning my times tables, but in this school, everyone was past that at my age. I knew nothing about Indian history – I didn't even know who Mahatma Gandhi was.

One of the biggest differences was how boys and girls relate to each other. In New Zealand, I took it for granted that I could look at or talk to girls and be friends with them. In India, you can't do that at all – but I learnt there were ways around it. In the late afternoon, my cousins and their friends would ride their motorbikes around the city. If my cousin liked someone and that girl was standing on the balcony of her house, he would ride past and they would just look at each other; this was their love story. Then they would do the same thing the next day. Sometimes a kid on the street would be asked to pass a note between them. I saw a lot of sneaky love stories that year – it was romantic, but it was also risky and, if discovered, the boy and girl could get into a lot of trouble. The guidelines for how to behave are strict and a person's reputation is extremely important. My cousins were fascinated by my stories about New Zealand, but they found it strange that you could go to a mall and talk to any girl, even one you didn't know. The questions they asked the most were: Can you hold hands? Can you hug? Can you talk and walk together in public?

Although I wasn't allowed to socialise with 'strangers' from school, I was always allowed to go out with family members. And in an Indian community, you don't really need friends as the extended family is so large. Even so, there were some people who looked at me differently because I was NRI. They thought I must be a spoilt brat to be flying around between countries. I was seen as privileged, my life in New Zealand was the one people in India aspired to so it didn't make sense to them that I would return to India. People assumed my family was wealthy because we were not in India, yet we didn't live a wealthy lifestyle in New Zealand terms.

My feelings about India changed a lot over the year. When I first arrived, I found it all a shock. I was not used to seeing so many people wherever I went, seeing such poverty, hearing car horns beeping constantly, and cows and other animals wandering on the streets. No one knows how great the difference between rich and poor can be until they go to India and see kids begging for money and sleeping on the footpaths. And I had been so attached to my parents – not even allowed to spend a night away from home on a sleepover – so I was confused that here they were pushing me away from them for a whole year. At first I just wanted to go back home. I had no friends, just cousins. I had no social life. I missed my parents a lot. There was no FaceTime for me to see and talk to them. I resented not having any freedom to go where I wanted away from family, like I could at home with my friends at the park.

But, gradually, I got used to it all. All my cousins were older than me so they looked after me, taking me for those rides on the motorbikes and to the shopping malls and they showed me a lot of love. Now it was the Indian family members who were growing very dear to me and I didn't miss my family in New Zealand so much. It seemed like no time at all and Mum was saying it was time to come back to New Zealand. This was not actually her wish. She would have liked me to stay at school in India until I graduated and for me to study to become an engineer. She thought I had a better chance of getting a qualification in India, but Dad and my uncle said it was time to rejoin my immediate family.

It was a difficult time. I was now accustomed to two very different families – my family in New Zealand and my relatives in India – but I had to leave India right when I had got close to everyone there. I wish my aunt and uncle could have come here to live, but they have their own lives in India. What was incredible was that my aunt came out to our wedding, as did one of my cousins, and it was so good to show them around and reconnect in person again. I can't wait to take Abbey and Noah to India one day. It will probably be our first overseas trip when we can travel after Covid, because I have been to Abbey's home country but she has never been to mine.

ABBEY

My mum is the most resilient person I know. She has been through so much and yet always remains positive, and is constantly working out ways to improve herself, which is a huge inspiration to me. I probably didn't realise at the time, when things were hard for me at school, that I was learning to be strong and resilient like her. When I began school in New Zealand, like Money, and pretty much any kid who looks or sounds different and is an outsider, I got bullied and teased at times.

In my hometown in Scotland, I had a good group of friends and we all got along really well. My best friend, Lizzie, and I spent the whole time together at school and on weekends. I went with her to Ireland in the school holidays once, and she came with us to Spain. We did everything together: dancing, playing, watching the Disney channel – just being kids. Everyone in the town knew each other. It was a very solid community, and I am still in touch with some of those friends from school days. Then, almost overnight, I was in New Zealand and we were finding a school near our rental, enrolling at it, buying the uniform. I was at the age where I was excited about everything and I wanted to get out there and make friends. Then the first day of school came around and on my way it suddenly hit me what I was about to do and I became so nervous I felt sick. My classmates had obviously been told a new student from Scotland was starting and they were all staring out of the classroom and watching me walk towards them, accompanied by a teacher. I had to find bravery inside me and face them as I walked in. I'll never forget it.

I was actually pretty happy at this school – which is crazy considering I left it a couple of years later – but I'm a social, friendly person once I feel comfortable in my surroundings, so I began making friends and throwing myself into school. But I remember one day my brother came back from the movies and he'd seen an advertisement for a new performing arts school. Students learn dancing and singing there, as well as their usual subject classes. He told Mum he needed to go to this school. He just wouldn't let up. Every day he was on at her. He used every argument he could think of, including the fact that this school used the Cambridge assessment system, the same UK qualifications he'd have received if he had been at school in Scotland. Also, because he is very creative, he wasn't getting on well at the regular state school we attended. Mum finally gave in and enrolled him in this expensive place.

Once he was attending it, every day he came home talking about how much fun he was having, and so, naturally, I started begging Mum to let me go as well. I had always wanted to dance. When I was in Scotland my sister and I learnt dancing and I loved it. 'Why can't I go too? It's not fair. I want to dance.' I went on and on. Mum ended up sending me there in Year 8 (when students are twelve and thirteen years old).

It was a small school with less than a hundred students. We had regular academic classes but got taken out of them for the dance lessons. That meant we had to catch up on our academic work in our own time. The school day started at eight in the morning and sometimes we were still there at nine at night. A dance class to start the day; dance classes during the day; more after school. It was crazy. I felt like I was almost living at that place. At first it was fun. We did ballet, jazz, contemporary, lyrical, hip-hop and character dance, a mixture of tap and ballroom. The teachers pushed us but were encouraging and I enjoyed the hard work.

I got much better at dancing and I liked being at the same school as my brother. But, being four years older than me, he soon graduated and was gone and then other things started to change. A lot of the old teachers left and were replaced by new ones – in fact, the staff turnover seemed to be alarmingly high.

I was not doing well academically and then my dancing began to suffer also. I tried my hardest but because of my body type, which was within the normal curvy range for my age group, I was always put in the back rows or made to dance with the younger kids. Other girls my age were getting solos and I wasn't going anywhere. I began to feel there was no point and I stopped trying. I felt I was wasting my time and my mum's money. It was an awful situation and a terrible time. Mum was working herself to the bone to send me there and I was messing around because I felt like the teachers didn't care about me. The pressure was coming at me from all sides. In my academic classes I was getting told off for falling behind and not doing enough. In the performance lessons, I was made to feel self-conscious about my size and that I shouldn't be eating or that I should eat less.

I wasn't the only one being picked on. My friend, Mollie, who had dyslexia, was told she was stupid. She got yelled at in class and given no extra help, even though her parents had specifically asked for her dyslexia to be taken into account when she enrolled. I remember another time, in the middle of a ballet class, in front of everyone, the teacher went up to a little girl who must have been about seven years old and yelled at her, 'Oh my God, you stink. Do you even shower?' But the most constant pressure was over our eating and body shape. It was so bad because it was happening at an age when many girls are already feeling so insecure about everything. And it didn't seem to matter what size we were.

The environment was so unhealthy and stressful. In partner work, where the boys lift the girls, I was never included. I'd have to go off and do group dances with others they didn't want in the class because of their size. They never said what the reason was, but we all knew and I would get so anxious when partner dances were coming up. I was insecure about everything. I wasn't chubby, but I thought I was fat because the others were all much skinnier than me. No matter how much I tried, I stayed curvy. In hindsight, I don't think any of us had a healthy relationship with food or our bodies, but how could we when the example being shown was so negative?

I wasn't even in a real ballet company where people would see me on stage. I was at a performing arts school to learn how to dance and do school work. I used fake tan – even at such a young age – to try and fit in with the other girls or avoid being made fun of because I am so pale. Where others could brown when sunbathing at the beach, I couldn't. I became more and more worried about showing my pale skin so I would cover myself up in dance classes. I was just a big bundle of insecurities. That is why now, on social media, I feel a real responsibility to show girls it is okay to be who they are, that there's no such thing as 'perfect'. I want to use this platform to help others and to remind them that a lot of these pictures they see aren't real but are using lots of filters and makeup.

The school ended up closing down, and I don't know of anyone from there who actually went on to have a career in the performing arts.

Finally, I was able to leave the school and go back to a state school in Year 12. But the difficulties didn't end there, because even though the arts school was emotionally tough, I'd made the best friends there and we were close – we still are. Now it was a new school, again. Everyone already had their friend groups, and although I had been to primary school with some of these students, I hadn't kept in contact so had lost those connections. Like anyone at that age, I worked hard to fit in. All you want is to be popular. I ended up getting into a really bad crowd that were into drinking and parties and skipping classes. I tried to do what the cool kids did but wasn't accepted by them either. What I do remember, on one positive note, is that I took dance as an option and it was the only time I had exposure to Indian dance before marrying Money, because we learnt different cultural styles every term and one of our guest teachers was a Bollywood dancer who taught us an Indian dance. I loved it so much, even if it was a one-off.

I felt like an outsider. All the time. I had never fitted in anywhere during my whole time at school. It was exhausting. Moving around so much hadn't helped, but it was more than that. It was like I couldn't do anything right. It got to the point where I locked myself in a toilet cubicle to eat my lunch or have a cry before my next classes. Worst of all, the school refused to do anything about the bullying. When I finally told Mum how bad it was she made an appointment to see them. My friend's father came along as a support person, which was so nice of him. Mum explained to them the whole story and what was going on.

'What do you want us to do?' was their response.

'Something,' urged Mum. 'Talk to these girls. I don't care what you do, but please do something.'

'We don't get involved in teenage dramas.'

Then my friend's dad went off at them: 'This girl is depressed. She is missing out on her education. She will have to move school if you won't deal with it.'

'Sorry. There is nothing we can do.'

It was insane. They thought I was either overreacting or that I'd brought it on myself.

These days, there is much more emphasis on speaking up about bullying, using counsellors at school is supported and mental-health issues are treated with much more care. But back then, I was made to feel like it was somehow my fault and I'd just need to get over it or fix it myself. It is almost unthinkable, but this is what it was like, only a few years ago.

With that lack of help from the school, and the relentless pressure I'd been under now for a number of years at both schools, I got to the point where I was in an extremely dark place and felt completely helpless and at times I wondered if it was worth carrying on. When I finally realised I had to reach out and I confided in Mum, she didn't waste any time. Feeling desperate herself, she took me to a mental-health facility for young people up to the age of eighteen. It was all fully funded, with really good psychiatrists on hand. The first one I spoke to dragged it all out of me – it felt so good to unload, at last.

'Who else do you need to hear this?' she asked. Of course, I said my mum, and I retold the whole thing to her, with the psychiatrist there for support. It can't have been easy for her to hear. Mum wanted to do whatever was needed straightaway, and she was upset, saying she hadn't realised how bad it was. But to be fair, she was at work a lot and not there when I got home from school, so she wouldn't see me come into the house crying. I had definitely been hiding it from her. I think a lot of people do that, so even if she had been around she might not have known. But I knew I couldn't keep living this way – eating my lunch in the bathroom at school or pretending I had gone to school but actually sneaking back home and staying there all day after Mum had left for work.

One day, she came home and found me there. She had been getting calls from school about my truancy and she was angry. It was ironic that the school was chasing us up over attendance when it was attending school that was the problem. Mum wanted to know why I was not going to school, but I wasn't upfront with her. I wish I had told her sooner. I don't know, sometimes you're so afraid to tell your parents what is going on. In the end, telling her everything was a massive weight off my shoulders, and she was immediately there to give me all the help I needed. I was given some medication for depression, as well as melatonin to help me sleep, which made a huge difference because I hadn't been sleeping well for ages. I received such good help there. I was finally starting to talk about things and people were finally starting to listen.

I begged Mum to let me change schools. The issue was, I only had half a year of official education left so no school really wanted to take me, they didn't see the point for such a short time. But Mum knew how bad things were; I was clinically depressed. I wouldn't come out of my room. I wouldn't go out with the friends I did have. Mum told the new school that I couldn't go another day where I was and she insisted on them enrolling me. Once they understood how serious it was, they were very accepting and said I could start the following Monday. The first person I was introduced to became my friend and I ended up joining her friend group. I felt accepted. Even for just half a year, that school was the right place for me and it made a big difference. I am still friends with those people – a couple of them were my bridesmaids at my wedding, and they love Noah.

Sometimes we don't realise the strength we have inside ourselves. And it is always better to seek help and talk about problems, no matter how hard it is to begin. Even if I knew some of what I had to say was hard for Mum to hear, it was better out; it was better said than bottling it up inside. I've learnt so much about not letting things get to me – and now I speak up when times are tough and I ask for help. It just took me a while to get there.

CHAPTER FOUR

Money's Teenage Years

MONEY

I returned to New Zealand but so much that had been familiar to me had changed. My friends were no longer hanging out at the park, some had moved to other schools, and it was like we'd matured at different rates. I didn't have any cousins with motorbikes to take me places. But I'm still grateful my parents made the year I spent in India happen; it confirmed a lot of things for me. Growing up in New Zealand, everyone was always busy whereas I learnt what family means in India. Another big influence on me was seeing the reality of poverty up close. I'm pleased with how I handled everything and got used to it all and stuck it out for the year. It taught me a lot about myself and helped my confidence.

Apart from that one year, all my schooling was on the North Shore. When I'm out with Abbey these days I often bump into someone else I went to school with, and she asks me, 'Did the whole of Auckland go to the same school as you?' It's funny but there do seem to be a lot of us still around this area, which is cool. Abbey and I have already discussed that we want Noah to go to co-ed schools. We feel it is important for him to get used to being around other genders, and we see co-ed schools as good environments for opening up, and understanding the world and how people are.

Friends are so important at that age and I was lucky that I made lots of them, particularly seeing it was now halfway through the next school year in New Zealand when I came back. On my first day, when I didn't think I would know anyone, I walked into class and a boy called out 'Money!' It was my old friend Diego.

I wasn't that smart a student. My English wasn't at the level it needed to be. Somehow, every time I read a book, the words go into my brain but my understanding doesn't keep up. I like books with pictures, because then I understand more of what is being said. It's like I don't seem able to turn words into pictures in my head for me to visualise them. I don't think I have ever read a complete book (except this one, of course). I did ESOL and I can read and write okay, in both English and Punjabi, and in India, I read books in Punjabi to help me learn the language. At the temple in Auckland, there are two screens, one on the men's side and one on the women's side. This helps me a lot because text is written in Punjabi script, then an English translation is provided below. For instance, it might say '*Ek Onkar*' in Punjabi, with 'One God' below it. I have found that this has helped me with the language.

By the time I was becoming a teenager, I felt we were becoming assimilated, living our Sikh life alongside our New Zealand life. There were still a few areas where this came into conflict, such as my parents' sleepover rule. Even when we had school camps, I wasn't allowed to go because that was counted as a sleepover. It sucked. And when everyone came back to school, all anyone would talk about was the fun and adventures they had had at camp while I had been back at school sitting in a classroom with the younger kids. The sleepover issue was big for me. In Year 9, one of my friends who lived just one street away was having a sleepover and I was invited with about four other kids. Mum told me I could go but she must have thought I was going to be home that night. I don't know if Dad wasn't paying attention or what the reason was, but just after nine o'clock there was a knock on the door and it was my dad.

'Come home, Money,' he said, in front of everyone.

I was so angry and embarrassed. 'What? You told me I could have a sleepover.'

But he wouldn't give in. I later found out that it was for the very Indian reason that there weren't just boys there – my friend had a sister, so that made it wrong in their eyes. I hated that rule and I've never forgotten that incident.

Dad was now drinking quite heavily. Back in India he never touched alcohol; he only started when he got to New Zealand. And he didn't drink at home, but he did after work, and that meant drinking and driving was a risk and I used to worry he might not come home one night. Sometimes, he would drive home and sit in the car at the end of the driveway and have a bottle or two of beer before coming inside. He was never abusive, just a quiet drinker, but Mum was very sensitive about it. She would get upset if he came home drunk, and I didn't like seeing her that way. Even today, if there is a social gathering with alcohol, the men will go off and drink on their own, not in front of the children, women or old people. These days, everything has changed with Dad and he's a one-Kingfisher-beer man, but growing up it was always an issue that lurked in the background.

Concerns about me being introduced to alcohol or girls or cigarettes were all behind my mother's refusal to let me stay over at friends' houses. She was happy for me to have them come to ours, but I was worried the house might smell of curry. It's crazy I thought this because when I was older, friends really wanted my mum's food. They would often ask if they could come to my house and sometimes they'd help me on my paper run if it meant they could come home for an Indian feed afterwards.

It dawned on me that I really liked having work and I was often checking out ways I could earn money. The first job I had was strawberry picking, but that was only for one day because they found out I was underage. But I saw that it was good to have a job. Another time, I taught ice-skating, even though at first I didn't know how to skate. I knew how to rollerblade and figured ice-skating was pretty much the same thing, so I taught myself when there was an ice rink set up at the local mall. The only thing I could do was skate fast, and turn on an angle to stop, and I suffered a few falls trying to learn. The woman who ran the rink saw me one day in the school holidays and asked if I'd like a part-time job.

'I'd love one,' I said.

'We would like you to train our younger skaters.'

I couldn't believe it – I didn't need a CV or anything. And teaching kids felt relevant.

Another time I had a job selling KiwiSaver. It was just starting up and they had a door-to-door sales campaign; I'd get a commission each time I managed to sign people on. I was quite young, just sixteen, but the woman obviously thought I would be good and she came to our house to get my parents' permission. I liked the work. I had confidence and it turned out I was a pretty good salesman.

I gave everything a go in any job I had and whatever was happening at school. I had dreams of being famous – it didn't matter whether it would be at sport or music or anything. Some friends and I decided to start a dance group, a mash-up of hip hop with a bit of contemporary; Chris Brown and the Pussycat Dolls were in there somewhere, but we practised heaps and performed at assembly. I was the worst, but we still did it. And by now I knew I preferred doing things rather than studying, so I chose practical subjects, but they didn't help me get any qualifications, and my parents didn't know how to make the necessary enquiries or check on me. I don't think it would ever have occurred to them. They relied on me to make the right choices and to know what I was doing.

'Are you doing well in your studies?' they'd ask.

'Yes, I am.'

'Are you doing your homework?'

'Yes, I am.'

They never checked. As long as I said I was passing the year and I showed them a result card, they didn't mind. I kept taking the practical subjects. I chose mechanical automotive as an option. My teacher was really great at working on cars and building things and so I learnt heaps from him. I chose food technology and learnt how to cook. I did music. I did woodwork classes where we made boats, or cut, sanded and prepared wood. I also liked life class that taught us skills such as how to put together a CV. I went for anything that looked like it would be easy credits. The only 'smart' subject I enjoyed was maths. I was okay at that, but I wasn't clever enough for science, I had no interest in history, and my English writing and grammar were weak. However, the easy credits weren't enough for me to pass the last year of school. I would have to worry about that later. For now, I wasn't too worried. I was just enjoying being young, spending time with friends and earning money.

Then I began working at The Warehouse, through a transition program where I got to try out retail experience, and I really liked the job and the place. I enjoyed the customers, I liked selling stuff, and I appreciated the variety and moving around different departments. I started as a checkout operator, moved to the various departments – I was even the fragrance seller at one stage. I was good at that; around Christmas time I sold perfume like candy.

When I was eventually made checkout supervisor, it was more challenging because I was overseeing people often older than me, and that generation didn't like younger ones telling them what to do. It wasn't easy, but it was what I was hired to do. But who would have guessed The Warehouse was going to play such a major role in what was about to unfold in my life?

CHAPTER FIVE

Love on the Shopfloor

ABBEY

In 2014, when I was seventeen, I was still at school but working part-time as a checkout operator at The Warehouse. I began in September when they took on casual staff to train them up before Christmas, and I soon got plenty of work. Before this, the only work I'd done was when my mum did independent midwifery and I was her office cleaner once a week, but I wasn't very good at it. They suggested I find another job, and that is how I ended up at The Warehouse.

Money was working there as a checkout supervisor, but I didn't meet him for a while, even though I heard about him. One of the other girls had a big crush on him. A really big crush. 'There's this guy called Money, and he's really dreamy,' she kept telling me. 'He's so much fun. We all really like him.' But I didn't know much else about him, and being quite shy and lacking confidence, I wasn't going to go out of my way to find out about him. I was just concentrating on learning the ropes at work.

It was also some time before we met because we always seemed to be on different shifts. But then, I saw him. Honestly, I thought he was the most good-looking guy I'd ever seen, so the physical attraction for me was there straightaway. As for his personality, I would say he was certainly cocky, but I really liked him – I just pretended he wasn't my type. Money had a reputation around The Warehouse as being this real flirty guy; he was always being cute and cheeky with customers and with his co-workers. Money was very different then to what he is now. Sometimes it is hard to believe he is the same person, but back then he'd put his arms around girls, he called everyone 'baby'. He was a classic. He never actually hit on anyone, there was a big difference between the way he talked and the way he acted, and he never gave anyone a reason not to trust him. It's just he was always so confident and outgoing and made everyone feel special. Like moths to a bright light, we kind of all wanted his attention.

But I totally believed he didn't like me because while he was full of jokes and banter around the others, with me he hardly said a word. In the staffroom, we'd glance at each other and quickly look away, and even when he had to give me instructions, he would be almost cross about it, compared to how he was with the rest of the team. Other staff seemed to be more onto us than we were, and when they saw us working alongside each other they used to say, 'Oh, you two are definitely going to get together. We can tell.'

I thought this was crazy. 'No way, not going to happen. He is so annoying. He's always telling me off.'

One time, I remember he told me quite crossly to fix my uniform as my skirt was too short, and I was surprised and embarrassed, and thought, *Okay, he really doesn't like me. I'll just try and forget about him* … but I don't know, *maybe* I would look out for him around the store and make a point of going down the aisle where he was working, and *maybe* I spent a bit longer getting ready before work in the mornings in case we did bump into each other …

MONEY

When I first met Abbey, we didn't hit it off straightaway, like we were on different wavelengths. Also, I think her friends had told her about my Indian background and that I had strict parents who would never let me date or marry outside my culture, so the idea of anything romantic between us probably never entered her mind. And it was true, I never thought of dating someone from outside my culture. If my parents didn't want me to date or marry someone, I wouldn't. They were only interested in setting up an arranged marriage when the time was right.

I had plenty of girls as friends, but I knew I couldn't be serious about any relationship that my parents hadn't arranged. This meant I probably came across as cocky and uncaring. In my mind, I was trying to be like Joey in the TV series *Friends*, with his 'How you doin'?' attitude. I thought he was the coolest guy.

A lot of young Indian guys, with their hair styled and brands on point, were expecting and wanting to be looked at. I had been working on this image since school. I was sure of myself and I liked being funny and enjoyed people liking me. And I loved my job and felt I was doing well. I got on with management, with my colleagues, older people, boys and girls my age – but Abbey was different. I knew there was something special about her. She was quite shy but she knew what she wanted and wasn't impressed by my 'cool' act. I wanted to be around her more and more, but I couldn't make it obvious. I actually didn't want her to think I was that guy, but I was a bit stuck with the character I'd been putting on for a while now. I could joke with others, but with her, I grew quiet. We'd be in the staffroom, never sitting near each other, but we kept catching each other's eye and looking away.

As the checkout supervisor, one of my tasks was organising the roster, so I started making sure we had our breaks at the same time. It just meant I could talk to her without being interrupted by work, and slowly we began chatting more. And I never talked in that jokey, flirty way to her, because I didn't want her to think I was just after a good time. Abbey would sometimes work on the shopfloor emptying pallets. I knew that if I was rostered on at the music department, the night before I'd work out a playlist of songs that hopefully she would hear as she was working, and they all had messages in them about romance and love. She had great legs, which others probably noticed too, and so I told her (from a management perspective, of course) that her skirt was too short because I didn't want others looking at her legs! I thought I was managing to be really sneaky and clever, but only later I realised it was one of those situations where everyone knew what was going on except us.

ABBEY

After a while, I could tell there was something between us. We'd find ourselves in the same areas in the store, often, or I would invent reasons to have to find him with a work query.

We were becoming more comfortable chatting together and I liked the Money I was seeing. In fact, I *really* liked him. Sometimes I'd get to my checkout counter to start work and there would be a little note left for me from him, always signed with a dollar sign. It was so cute. I still have some of those notes. By February, Money finally asked me out on a date. Well, not really a date. He asked me to go out, but in a group with him and his friends, and I said no. I didn't want to be 'one of the boys' who just happened to be a girl. I wasn't interested in being in his 'gang'. So that was that.

Money kept the banter and flirting going at work, but I think he was scared of doing anything that looked like a date. He kept asking though, and when I did eventually agree to go out with him, it was with his friends. He pointed out that it was easier for him to go to parties because it meant when his mum asked where he was going he could say he was with friends and be telling the truth. It was a sneaky way of making the two worlds meet. One night when we were at this party, I found out once and for all that he had a genuine interest in me, because two of his friends were hitting on me, not knowing that I was only there because of Money, and it was awkward as he hadn't told them and was introducing me as his friend from work. Then he told them to stay away. That night he asked if I wanted to go out on an actual date, just with him, and that happened a week later.

We talked so much on our first date, connecting really quickly. We both have strong family values and we found ourselves talking about every important facet of our lives going forward: that we both liked and wanted kids, where we saw ourselves in the future, how it mattered to build strong foundations straightaway and what our ideal family would look like. Hitting it off like this so quickly just reinforces that even coming from different cultures, humans are not really that different from each other. Everyone wants to be loved. It was crazy how much we had in common. We even agreed that when we bought a house we both intended living near our parents so that our kids – which we talked about wanting – would live close to their extended family. It was hypothetical – but it was meaningful.

I was surprised at how much we shared, because in my mind he was potentially still this cocky person from work, but here I was seeing a completely different side to him and discovering he wanted all the things I wanted. I got home and thought, *I can't believe I talked to someone about all of that on a first date.* I was worried I had talked too much and then was worried he wouldn't want to have anything more to do with me, in case I'd frightened him off. As I was on my way home, my phone pinged and it was a text from him. My heart raced. *Good,* I thought, *he's already contacting me!* until I read it and he was saying maybe we should take things slowly. Often, when we're still unsure, early on in a relationship, we decide what things mean without checking or talking about it first. So I decided in my head this meant he wasn't interested after all and perhaps I'd opened up too much and he didn't like that or he didn't like me. It was only later I learnt that he was scared of his emotions and of what his family would say and he didn't really know what to do with everything that was happening.

Of course, I played it cool and didn't reply. But that was confusing because the next day at work we had a shift together and he had already told people we had been on a date, and all the younger girls came running over wanting to know what it was like. I was so embarrassed because I was sure he'd have told them he wasn't that interested. I could hardly look at him. And because we were both so nervous about stuffing it up, when what we had seemed too good to be true, we began playing games with ourselves and second-guessing: *Do I text back? Do I wait a few days?* Rather than being honest and saying 'I really like you and we should go out', we stayed scared and distant.

MONEY

We kept it on the down-low at work – or at least we thought we did. I'd sneak notes onto her cash register before she got into work, or we'd just happen to find ourselves hanging out in the same aisle as if we both needed to be there, and we would be in the staffroom together on breaks. I was nervous in case the managers found out because we couldn't afford to lose our jobs, and yet work was when we could be together. But it turned out it wasn't a problem – there were other couples working at The Warehouse and it was perfectly fine. We went on our first holiday together to the Coromandel, which was incredible. But without thinking, we'd both applied for leave for exactly the same dates – and we hadn't thought the managers would click? When Abbey eventually told one of our bosses, he just said, 'Oh yeah, we've all known about this for months.'

The biggest issue wasn't work; it was what my family would say. Getting their approval for a *love* marriage as opposed to an arranged marriage within my culture would have been difficult enough, but marriage to a European girl was just out of the question. And it didn't just stem from prejudice or my parents' rules. I didn't know if Abbey would understand my culture or appreciate it. It was like me worrying about bringing friends home to a house that smelt of curry, but 100 times worse. And I forgot that, as it happened, my friends really liked the food. I had certainly never dated openly before, but I didn't realise issues would arise no matter what cultures the two people belong to. But for as long as I can remember, Mum had told me I would have an arranged marriage to a

Punjabi girl. She'd always say, 'Promise me, Money, you will never drink'; 'Promise me you will agree to an arranged marriage and we'll have a traditional Punjabi wedding.' And I would agree, even though I didn't necessarily want one in my heart. But it wasn't about what I wanted. I had seen so many family dramas play out in Indian households by now that, subconsciously, I didn't even want to date a Punjabi girl. I couldn't handle all the pressures placed on us within the Indian community and I just tried to not think about it.

As kids, we'd witness family members fighting. It was mainly miscommunications and living as a joint family that caused the most tension as no one had their own space. There were some arguments that got really bad, with people being abusive and swearing and my mum would always take it to heart. When she got really upset she would cry so much she couldn't breathe and would end up going to hospital. She'd remind my dad that he had his whole family here, while hers had been left behind in India. I couldn't detach myself from it because I was so close to Mum. She would be crying and gasping and I would be praying.

I had no idea what to do. It started to look like I wanted to date Abbey and spend more time with her, but I was caught in the middle – the kind of marriage I was allowed was not one I wanted, and the kind I wanted was not one I was allowed.

A love marriage versus an arranged marriage is a huge issue in our culture. When you seek a love marriage, parents have no control over it like they do when it is arranged. Part of the reason it is so important is that a bride (usually) comes to live with her husband's parents, and so it is not just him that's marrying her – it's like everyone is marrying her. There are lots of subtleties to the whole thing. For instance, I know of two of my cousins who had love marriages, but their families turned those into arranged marriages. My cousins found someone they wanted as their life partner, they told their parents, who then met with the girl's parents early on. The sets of parents agreed and took it from there as though it had been the parents' arrangement all along. They flipped it around to look like an arranged marriage, so it could be approved within the community, and no one knew till much later on that my cousins had been the ones who initiated it. That happens quite a lot because Indian families care so much about how things will appear and other people's opinions.

The next generation after ours will be even more liberal and Western in their thinking. We can already see this happening in the time Abbey and I have been together, and it is awesome. The community is being introduced to all sorts of different ways of doing things – and they see this happening online and overseas. For instance, people in

India are seeing Indian communities in various countries experiencing love marriages, and they are asking why they can't, too. If you love someone, you should be able to marry them without huge arguments and all this angst, and you should be able to embrace each other's culture and people should trust in the two people involved.

An arranged marriage is not a forced marriage; in an arrangement, a person is not forced to marry someone they don't want to. Many couples and families still prefer this traditional way. A lot of my cousins say they go along with it because it's easier and less responsibility on them. That's perfect if it works for them. In the end, marriage is marriage, whether it is arranged or a love match. Couples still have the same problems and still have to work them out together. But with love matches you do have more knowledge of the person you are about to marry because of the time spent together – you should know by then what they stand for, and you tend to know whether you could make it work. With arranged marriages, you don't know anything until it starts happening.

Covid and immigration rules create other complications. If I hadn't met someone, my parents would have found me a girl, probably back in India. I would have gone there to marry her. For me to come back to New Zealand as a citizen would have been fine if I could secure managed isolation, but then there would be a whole lot of processes to go through to get her here to join me. Couples can be married and spend years apart waiting for the official signoff. We have a friend in exactly that position and it is very sad. In their whole marriage so far they have spent only a couple of months together. And Covid has meant that even if her residency were approved, she would still not be able to come here under these New Zealand border restrictions.

If I had not met Abbey, I wasn't just going to find any girl to prove a point. I would have had an arranged marriage, and it might have worked out, or it might not have. I might have been emotionally scarred, as some people are, by being with a partner every day and having to pretend to love them. You eventually get there, I think. But, after all her opposition in the early days, my mum has told Abbey and me that she is grateful for our relationship because it is true love. She and my dad can see we really love each other and they couldn't even imagine anybody else for me but Abbey now. Yet, if I want to know whether arranged marriages can work, I only have to look at my parents, who also love each other very much.

When Abbey and I began dating, I would tell my parents I was at work, but I would go to Abbey's house, which was a 10-minute drive from work, and we would watch a movie together and hang out. I left my house with my uniform on and a bag containing a change of clothes for our date.

We had some close shaves. Sometimes Mum called me and asked, 'Where are you?'

'I am at work.'

'But I just went there to see you, and they said you weren't there.'

'Oh, I was out the back. The person you spoke to wouldn't have known that.'

'We couldn't see your car – we looked for it.'

'I thought I told you, I'm not at the usual store tonight. They asked me to go and help at another location.'

It was awful playing these games and lying like this. At times I asked the manager to cover for me if my parents called the store while I was at Abbey's place. A lot of our co-workers were involved in what was going on and helped make excuses for us. It was like we were teenagers again, when you'd each make an agreement with a friend to say you were staying at that person's house as a cover. I was quite lucky that some of the managers I worked with were of Indian descent, guys who were trying to get their own permanent residency and live a life of freedom away from their families, so they knew what was happening with me and were happy to do what they could to help keep up this charade. But

Mum said later, when all of this came out, that she knew something was going on, that I was working very hard to keep someone secret, she just didn't know who the girl was. Night-filling shelves was also an excellent cover because that took place after the store had closed, with shifts lasting till five in the morning, so it was a perfect excuse, and there was no chance my mum would pop in to see me then.

By now, Abbey's mum knew me quite well and was used to seeing me run out the door at the end of the evening to return home, putting my uniform back on – a bit like Superman changing from Clark Kent – but it would have been too weird to have gone on a date with Abbey while still dressed in my Warehouse uniform.

ABBEY

Money didn't tell his parents about us until we had been together for five or six months. By the time he did, we knew each other very well, but our relationship was still secret from them. If we went on a date, I would park two streets from his house and text him to come and meet me. And we never went anywhere on the North Shore because with so many of his family members in the area, the chances of being seen were high. Our first proper date together with just the two of us was at a restaurant called Caravanserai, in the city centre, and it is still our favourite place to go for special anniversaries.

But the funniest thing, and it always reminds me of those romantic comedy films, is that his family were regular customers at The Warehouse. I knew who they were, but they had no idea about me.

'Do you know our son Money who works here?' his mother would ask me.

'Oh yes, I think so,' I said, hoping my voice wasn't trembling.

His mum came in a lot when he was working. It was really hard. She would come to my checkout every time – it was almost as though she knew, even though she didn't. I would be shy and awkward, scanning her shopping through and thinking, *You don't know I'm dating your son*, and how terrified I would be if she found out. And she was always really nice to me. I felt so guilty in my heart; I kept thinking, *I am keeping this massive secret from you and you are such a sweet lady.*

It took a long time for Money and me to start calling each other boyfriend and girlfriend. Sometimes before then we'd be out and because we weren't actually 'official', boys might try to chat me up. 'So are you single?' they'd ask.

I looked at Money. *Was I*?

'She's with me,' he'd say.

Was I? Okay. Good to know.

I had told my mum about Money before our first date. I am lucky that I have a really open relationship with her. She had absolutely no problem with me dating someone from a different culture; she just wanted me to be happy and to be comfortable with the decisions I was making.

'And his name's Money,' I said.

'Oh, that's a cool name.'

She met him very early on. Actually, when he picked me up for our first date, I had even asked, 'Do you want to come in and meet my mum just quickly?'

'Not really.' He looked shocked. Then a couple of weeks later he came in, although he was still nervous. He had never met a girlfriend's parents in his life – not that he had ever dated anyone seriously before me. I'd explained that my mum was very different to his and was relaxed about the whole thing, but he was worried there would be disapproval at some level. When there is no dating and marriages are arranged, there are no rules about what to say or do when you meet a girl's parent in this situation. 'Hi, Mum' was the first thing he said, and he gave her a hug. This would be expected of him according to Indian culture, where you address your friend's parents the way they address them, so, Mum, Dad, Aunty, and so on. You never call them by their first name. Mum was a bit surprised at first, but then she thought it was really sweet. In fact, she thought he was really sweet in general and the meeting went well. She told me she liked him straightaway, which meant a lot to me. Deep down, we want our parents' approval, even if we know it won't affect our decisions. It helps, though. It calmed my nerves and made me feel like I was making the right choice. It was extra important for me that she like him because I have so little family here. I needed everyone to get on because there'd be no one else to turn to if they didn't. He soon became a favourite with her.

Mum is very open-minded, and I have always been fascinated by other cultures and enjoyed learning about them. Mum told me that if someone in our family was going to become involved with another culture, it would be me. Our town in Scotland, Bellshill, is not particularly multicultural and back then it was quite small, with only about 40,000 people living there. There were some immigrants, quite a few from Pakistan, but there was very little integration between them and the locals. It's a shame, but I understand it a lot more now. I see that it would have been easier for the Pakistani newcomers to stay within their own community, and they probably experienced the same difficulties Money's parents did arriving in New Zealand, having to learn to speak the language and learn the new culture. There's so much more a 'home' population needs to do for migrants arriving to a new country. But, I know I didn't grow up being exposed to other cultures and I remember noticing how much I liked the more multicultural New Zealand.

When I got together with my Punjabi boyfriend, Mum was almost expecting it, but Money had been keeping this cultural side of himself so well hidden that I didn't even know he was from India. It was ages after we'd been working together and I remember I picked up his CV that was coming off the printer in the staffroom. I saw on the top page that he was born in India.

'You never told me you're Indian,' I said. 'That's so cool. How come you haven't mentioned this?' I asked him so much about it and straightaway wanted to understand and get to know this side of him. Since we've been together, Money always credits me with getting him back in touch with his Punjabi culture and him having a renewed respect for his family. He liked becoming a more respectful person in general. I knew it was there; he had just got used to hiding it.

CHAPTER SIX

Getting Ahead

ABBEY

I didn't have a game plan in terms of a career. I knew, having failed my last year at school, Year 13, I would have to do some sort of catch-up if I wanted to do tertiary study, but I wasn't ready to do that straightaway, so decided to take a gap year. Mum was supportive. She thought it was a good idea to be sure and know what I wanted, rather than go to university because it's what I was supposed to do. Since I was already working at The Warehouse, I decided to take on one of their full-time positions after school finished.

The Warehouse is a great place for a young person starting out in work. You learn so much that is important. You have to be committed and turn up, be on time, interact and get on with all sorts of other people. I liked my co-workers, we had a good time at work and the pay was pretty good. I had tried out every part of the store, from cashier to handling returns, to working on the shopfloor. When I went full time, Money cautioned me: 'A lot of people start working here as a gap year and are still working here in their fifties. It's easy to get complacent and just cruise, then before you know it, it's too late to do anything else. Remember you are supposed to also think about what you really want to do.'

This was also the year I met Money's parents, but I'd been learning about his culture and preparing myself for the meeting by then. And at the end of the year, I was ready to focus on where I wanted to take my career, which was something around psychology and mental health. In the meantime, I got to hang out with Money at work, we'd go to the gym together and we went on holidays – they were meant to be a secret, but probably weren't. There were about forty people working at The Warehouse, with a core group of twenty of us who worked the same hours every day. It was great fun.

I was one of the younger full-time staff members, as well as my friend Sarah who'd got me the job. Some of the older ones scared me at first. They were set in their ways and it was quite intimidating; they'd worked there for such a long time. It was tough for someone like me who isn't the most assertive person in the world. There were three elderly staff members who worked on the checkouts and had been there for about thirty years. They were happy doing what they were doing. It was social for them and they had no interest in moving up the ladder. But I was keen to learn as much as I could and soon I was made a checkout supervisor. These women actually supported Money and me in our relationship, and they weren't being mean to me, they just didn't want me bossing them around. And me being the sort of person I am, if I asked them to do something and they ignored me or said no or came up with some excuse such as 'I've got a sore knee', I backed down.

'Okay,' I'd say. 'Don't worry – you take it easy till you feel better. I can do it.' I didn't argue. I would just do whatever the chore was myself. Then I would get in trouble with the boss for not insisting they do it, but to me it was easier than trying to take them on. I'm not cut out to be a supervisor. I shouldn't be expected to boss people around or be in charge; it isn't in my nature. Fortunately, management figured that out too, and found other things for me to do.

Money and I have had this strange habit of doing things independently yet at the same time. There was us working at The Warehouse, and both failing to get university entrance qualifications at school. Then we ended up doing a foundation course at the same place together.

It shouldn't have been a surprise that I failed Year 13, considering all I had been through, with so much disruption, changing schools, finding friends, and dealing with my depression, and I had tried to cope with it all on my own for so long. It had been a tough time and I think by Year 13, I had run out of energy. Before then I'd done quite well and managed to get some good grades. I was probably lucky to get any education at all. It was also in Year 13 when I began at The Warehouse and sometimes I skipped classes to do shifts there, which wouldn't have helped my chances of passing.

'You know you want to go to uni,' Money kept saying to me that year, 'you have to make it happen.'

I wanted to study psychology because of my own mental-health struggles and because I wanted to help people. The foundation course would earn me enough credits in six months to enrol at university to study psychology and criminology. The course crams a year's worth of study into half a year. Money pushed me to do this and I am glad he did. I didn't really like the campus, but the course itself was fine. I had to work hard, but it was manageable, and I felt supported by the polytech. When you outline what it is you want to study at university, they put you into the appropriate foundation classes, which means you're prepared and ready to go when you get there.

I learnt things I had missed out on in high school: maths, science and English, as well as how to write essays and use references and all that. I passed with good grades and was excited for the next stage – my degree. I felt like my life was finally on track, I knew where I was going. It was great for my confidence. I had spent all those years not quite getting where I wanted to be. Then I was able to go and do this course, in six months, with no one helping me and being treated like an adult. I knew I wanted to get into university, I wasn't there to make friends or have fun. It felt good, different, like I was in charge of my own destiny.

I started the foundation course at the beginning of 2015, then applied for university at the AUT city campus in the second semester, in June. But I didn't hear back from them. According to their systems, my application had been processed but I hadn't received anything to confirm I could start my course or what to do about it. I spent a week refreshing emails – 'application processed'; 'application processed'; 'application processed'.

Money's patience ran out before mine. 'We're not taking this anymore,' he said. 'Come on. We are going in and you're going to talk to the admissions person face to face.'

This is something I would never have done by myself. But we did it. We found what looked like the right office and sat down and Money did the talking. 'My friend has applied, she's qualified, she keeps being told it's being processed. What is going on?'

And the woman just looked at my application and said, 'Okay, you are accepted. Start tomorrow.'

By this stage, everyone else had already been to orientation and were making some friends and knew where their lecture rooms were, so I felt a bit behind. I get self-conscious in these situations. I walked into my first class and all I could see were people sitting in their friend groups joking and chatting. I didn't know where to sit. I saw these two friendly-looking guys sitting together who smiled at me and seemed welcoming, so I went and sat with them. One of them is still my good friend to this day.

I had chosen to do a Bachelor of Arts, majoring in psychology and with a minor in criminology. For the first year there are also what felt like random subjects, such as a comms class – all we did was have conversations, first in small groups about the topic, then we debated them with other people. Somehow, I managed to pass all the classes, but it wasn't exactly what I had in mind. The course was more suited to someone wanting to be a research psychologist, learning how to write reports and do case studies. I had been imagining myself as a counsellor or hands-on psychologist. My dream job would be a police psychologist, helping people affected by crime. Many students dropped out or changed courses in the first year, but I stuck with it. I probably just chose the wrong course. A friend of mine did a bachelor's degree in counselling and walked straight into a job, making good money. But things improved as I continued along. In my last year I did a paper called Understanding Emotions, which was about mental health. I loved that class. I knew it was what I was interested in. I can proudly say I never failed one paper at university. I graduated in 2019, and a couple of weeks after that we found out I was pregnant. I love the thought that when I walked across the stage to accept my degree, Noah was with me – but that's jumping way ahead, and plenty happened before then!

MONEY

In my last two years at school I had done Gateway, a program that helps students transition into the workforce by placing them in a workplace a couple of days a week while still at school. It was hands-on experience and at first I worked at one of the Midas branches, in their automotive repairs workshop. I loved it and I passed the course. Because I like cars, I then took automotive engineering at Unitec for a year, but I realised it wasn't where my future lay. Part of the problem was that I found the work too dirty. I'm a really clean person. Also, my family wasn't very impressed.

'Why aren't you doing accounting?' asked my uncle. 'Or what about finance or law or real estate.' Any of these areas of study would have helped them, as by now they had started buying property. It's very much like my family to think like this, to choose a career that will benefit the whole family. The way I was heading, all I would be able to do is repair the family's cars from time to time.

'Are you sure you're enjoying this automotive?' my dad asked me. He always took what my uncle said on board. Eventually, their arguments got to me and when I quit the auto course, at the back of my mind was finding something to make my dad proud. So after I took the foundation course to make up for what I had missed at school, I enrolled in business at AUT. By this time, I was working part-time at The Warehouse, and putting in a lot of hours there.

But for AUT, I had to first get the basics in finance, accounting and economics. I failed a few papers and had to repeat them until I succeeded, and in the end I turned away from accounting and finance and moved into marketing and entrepreneurship. Then I passed everything and some of it I enjoyed – but I still don't have my degree. The final practical requirement of the course was a three-month work placement with a company, and I never got around to doing this, so, in a way I am in debt with a student loan and nothing to show for it. That wasn't showing good financial management or business sense.

Still, while I was at university, I discovered more ways to make money. I began making websites for people, using e-commerce sites. I searched online for companies that needed to upgrade their websites and I'd message them, offering to handle their social media and other online activities. Some took me up on this. I was still working at The Warehouse, which was such a good workplace for me – most of all because it is where I met Abbey – but I learnt heaps. I had to work with so many different people, manage staff, manage relationships and deal with customers on a daily basis. The Warehouse is a diverse-conscious employer and although I did have racism directed against me in person one time, I was learning all the time how to handle situations, how to work under pressure, how to not take things personally and stay positive.

Then I started an online second-hand vintage clothing store, which I'm sure was just an extension of the inorganic rubbish collections years earlier, but I was always into buying second-hand stuff because I knew what would hold its value. Vintage clothing wasn't as popular then as it is now but I worked hard on it for a year and it was great fun. I built up an audience through social media, then found suppliers in London and the US and brought in branded vintage clothing and big brand names. Or I'd buy items from the 1990s that I could get cheap and then sell for a couple of hundred dollars. I bought glasses on AliExpress that I could sell for double what I paid for them.

My company was run out of my bedroom in my parents' house. I had the room nicely laid out with the clothes presented and displayed. People could buy online, or come and try before they bought them. Then at night I would bring out my mattress and turn it back into my bedroom. My parents were proud of my ability to make money but didn't embrace it completely because it was second-hand. They thought my online business was okay, it was good I was making some money and that I was getting good experience, but really I should be aiming to get a job in a bank so that their friends could say, 'You must be so proud that your Money has a good job.' A job in a bank meant security and respect from others, as they were of that generation that opinions mattered and they cared how things looked. Basically, they really wanted me to do an office job, but spending my days working away in a little corner office somewhere was never me. But I couldn't tell them that. However, their ambitions did help me reach a good level at university, though that wasn't what they had intended.

Back in high school, my mother had wanted to get me into a 'good school' near us but we weren't in the residential zone for it. When it was Ash's turn, she again tried hard to get him enrolled there, with no success. Ash was in Year 11 then and was starting his NCEA levels. My cousin had moved here from India by now and I suggested that the family get a rental house in the Westlake zone, which my cousin and I would move into, and Ash too – then he'd be in the right zone. My mother liked that idea. She was doing it for my brother, but I was doing it for me. It was a master plan to get away from my parents and gain some freedom. And she wasn't worried about us because the new house was still close by them. I did so much business out of that rental property. I didn't have to use my bedroom as a shop any more as I'd made sure the house we found had a garage on the driveway, which we converted into the clothing store. The business did very well until I had had enough and it was time to move on to something else.

All of this makes me think about the immigration cycle of struggle that I have watched play out in different ways to this day. Young adults come here on student visas and they have to pay thousands in fees to study while hoping to gain residency and eventually bring their families over. In the meantime, there is all the pressure to pass exams and support themselves and save money for their family. But they are allowed to work no more than twenty hours a week and some struggle to pay for rent and food. When they finish studying, they have to move out of somewhere like Auckland to earn more points to get enough to earn residency. It shows how highly valued a life in New Zealand is. If those people stayed in India, for example, they wouldn't have to work so hard, but the work and opportunities wouldn't be there either. Here they have to do so much more to survive with the added pressure of knowing their parents are counting on them to succeed.

I remember when I was growing up, I'd get asked all the time: 'Does your family own a dairy?' I would be so defensive at this, thinking it would be awful if they did, and I'd immediately dispute it: 'My dad is a tailor. He doesn't work in a dairy.' Now that I'm older and understand more, I totally appreciate how much hard work there is in owning a dairy. It's a difficult job with long hours and lots of stress – but it also means that person can buy a home for their family. There are so many ways to get ahead.

CHAPTER SEVEN

The Showdown

MONEY

Abbey and I had been dating for about four months. What was about to happen had the potential of creating such a rift, I had to be sure we were both committed before I broke the news about us to my parents.

'I don't ever want to be with anyone but you,' I told Abbey. 'Do you feel the same way?'

She did. 'I love you, I'm here for you. I'm not going anywhere. I'm willing to fight for this,' she said.

At this point I was terrified; I'd almost convinced myself it wasn't going to work before I even tried. And I didn't want Abbey to have unrealistic expectations. 'Please don't get your hopes up. My parents are never going to agree to this,' I'd tell her. 'And if it doesn't work out, it is only because of them, not because I don't love you.'

There are two scenarios my parents would vehemently oppose: me having a love marriage rather than an arranged marriage, or, worse, me falling for someone who wasn't from our Indian culture. They were so sure that the girl wouldn't understand or follow their ways and might raise their future grandchildren to not know or follow them. My situation was more complicated because I was the eldest and the first in the family to get married, so what I did would affect many other lives. If I didn't abide by their preference, others would be given licence to not do so either, but if my parents stood in the way and stopped me, then the others would also have to step into line and respect the traditional way. I can see the results of this when I look at my brother's life now. He has it so easy in comparison. Ash can go out whenever he wants, he can go on sleepovers, he can date anyone he likes, regardless of who they are or where they are from. And I am happy for him. But all of this has changed in just five short years, because of what we fought for and what was about to go down in our family.

In about June, I told my mum I had met a European girl – and that was as good as saying I wanted to marry this girl. In our culture a relationship only results in marriage.

'I don't want to hear it,' said Mum. 'Don't even talk about it.'

All I could do was keep repeating it. 'Mum, I'm dating someone. You need to meet this girl.'

'I don't want to meet her. I don't want to know anything about her. I don't want to know who she is, where she works, where she lives. None of it.'

'Mum, please just listen to me!'

'If I know, I will want more information, and you will feel like I'm softening, which I'm not going to do. I won't let you do this.'

There was a lot of screaming and crying. Mum and I were either arguing or not speaking to each other for days at a time. It took a month before she agreed to meet Abbey. This was so hard on Abbey as well. I would come over to her mum's house and fill her in on the latest argument and what had been said, and she felt guilty for her part in this fight. She was trying to understand their views – and mine. I had to say to her, 'If it doesn't work out, and my mum says no, there is nothing I can do.' It killed me to say it but I knew I spoke the truth: 'If she doesn't agree, I'm sorry. I'm not going to leave my mother for you. Her happiness comes first. You have to know that.'

Although Mum was playing tough, it was hurting her too. We are a big part of each other's worlds. But there was no simple solution – someone would have to give in. Within our Punjabi community, what I was doing was more than going against tradition. How we uphold the culture within the community and what others think of us was more important to Mum and Dad than what they believed themselves. And even while Mum was the one I was trying to convince and she kept refusing to discuss it, she wasn't the one who was most opposed. Every time she tried to talk about the situation to my dad, he cut her straight off.

'I'm not talking about it. I don't want to have to discuss with my brothers what is happening. This cannot happen,' he argued. 'Stop bringing it up.'

He didn't want to risk the family's reputation and everything they had built for themselves here in New Zealand. That is the only thing he saw when he even thought about Abbey. We were ruining their lives. He refused to engage in a discussion about it, with me or my mother. My dad took a very long time to accept Abbey, and I understand this. He is the eldest brother so he is in charge of maintaining the family's standing. He has to lead the way. Dad doesn't just care what his brothers and sisters think of us. He cares about how society sees us. Our reputation is based on the values we show to the world: that we are family-oriented, that our culture matters, that we keep our heads down, work hard, follow our Sikh religion. They so strongly believe that if you marry an outsider, you are saying you are not going to be part of the culture any more, you won't go to the *Gurdwara* or speak Punjabi, and your kids won't speak Punjabi or be part of the culture.

There were other ways in which our traditions would get ignored if I married Abbey. Back in their day, but not so much anymore, the wife is in charge of the household. She is responsible for the cooking and cleaning and taking care of the household. I saw my mum take on this role when my uncles got married. She had to sort out everyone else's dramas and everyone's weddings. Everything is done by the female. As my wife, Abbey would be expected to take on that role too, so it was another reason to worry and stress: How would that person possibly fit in? How would they move in and fulfil those duties the way it had always been done?

My parents' solution was to threaten to send me back to India for an arranged marriage. This is the number one threat in my family when things aren't going well: 'We will send you back. We will show you how hard it is over there. You will see what we have given you and what you are throwing away.'

'Why did you bring me here if you don't want me to live my own life?' I kept shouting. 'Why won't you even meet the person I am in love with? This is who I want to be with.'

It was so horrible. It was such a lot of mental stress for Abbey and me. Sometimes I wonder how we even managed to get through it. We couldn't see when it would end – or how it would end.

ABBEY

You couldn't find more of a contrast than between our two families about our relationship. Mum was so happy for me, she liked Money and she could see that we were really good together. I am a really empathetic person, so even though I didn't have to experience what Money was going through, I felt terrible for him and really sad. It was one of the worst times of our lives. Every day there was another argument, another hurt; Money's parents were adamant they wouldn't give in and he was not able to reason with them. I wanted to see him and spend time with him like a regular couple would do when dating, but it couldn't happen. It was secretive, and we were pushed for time, and the way forward was all we ever talked about, with no end in sight. Sometimes it made the two of us argue as well, as I just wanted to be with him and have a normal relationship.

All along, I kept thinking, they'll come round, they'll be fine, until I began bracing myself for the worst, and had to imagine us breaking up. But somehow, I still felt optimistic we'd get there. While they argued, I did lots of research into the Sikh religion and Punjabi culture. I read and read about it and watched documentaries. I knew that if I ever met

Money's mother, Pam, I would have to prove to her that I was interested in their culture and willing to learn, or she wouldn't accept me. And I was happy to do this because I was so interested to know more. I learnt things about Sikhism even Money didn't know. He obviously understood his religion from growing up in it, so he had never had to study it, but I would ask him if he knew about the things I was learning. I remember we were discussing the Sikh surnames, how all men are 'Singh' and all women are 'Kaur', and he knew that Singh meant lion, but I said to him, 'Did you know that Kaur means princess and lioness?' I thought this was beautiful – and apt – as if his mum were protecting her cub from this foreigner invading their territory. Learning about Sikhism and their culture made me feel like a tourist; you visit the sights the locals never get around to because they're just there. The tourist reads up on everything, they stop to take note, they want to understand, whereas when you are inside the culture, often there is no questioning or real learning that happens; it's just part of you and you may not ever study it.

When Money's mum decided that she would see me, it was to tell me in person to stay away from her son. 'I'm going to tell her,' she told Money. 'You're not listening, so I will tell your girlfriend. I will meet her for five minutes.'

Thank goodness I didn't know all of this at the time – I wouldn't have been able to get out of the car. I've never been more nervous, but I was also excited. I couldn't believe we had managed a breakthrough, even if just this tiny opening. I arranged a gift as a thank you for her agreeing to meet me and to hopefully break the ice. I knew the Golden Temple in Amritsar was the central religious place of the Sikhs so I ordered a painting of it to give to Pam. It is a very special image with a lot of meaning behind it. It depicts the first and tenth Gurus of Sikhs looking down over the temple. I really hoped she would appreciate this gesture.

Money and I walked in together to where she was waiting for us at her house.

'Mum, this is Abbey,' he said.

'Hello, it's so nice to meet you,' I said, and I touched her feet (as is customary when greeting, in Punjabi culture) and she did give me a hug, so I thought that was a good sign. When I gave her the framed picture she was so shocked. She smiled at me and kept holding it and looking at it. I hadn't even told Money what I had planned to do so it was genuine disbelief on her face that I had gone to this effort. I think, in my heart, this was the moment I knew it might work because I saw love in her eyes as she thanked me. We exchanged just a few words. Money said we were going to the *Gurdwara* next and how I really wanted to see it, and I think she told me that I looked like a doll and was beautiful.

She took me into another room away from her son and I was so worked up I can hardly recall what happened, but I do remember some strong words from her, where she clearly stated that I was never to hurt her son as he had already fought so hard for me. It was all about protecting Money. I was quiet the whole time, but I thought it went well. I expected it to be much worse after all the build-up, actually. The visit probably took about ten minutes at the most. In the end, she wanted us to stay longer, but Money rushed me out of the house, he was so worried something could go wrong at any moment, which I totally understood. He also saw how nervous I was and just wanted to take some of the pressure off me. Once we were back in the car, I told Money his mum seemed very sweet, and that I could see us being close one day – which now we are. We love each other very much.

From one intimidating visit to the next, we went straight to Nanaksar *Gurdwara*, the temple in Manurewa. Again, I was trying my hardest every moment to know what to do, where to be, how to act. Because there are so few European people who visit the temple, there were hundreds of people staring at me, and apparently I had put my head covering on wrong, because a girl came up to me and told me I was not being modest in the *Gurdwara*. It was nerve-wracking, and yet I really wanted to understand as much as I could. It was incredible to see around the *Gurdwara* – I thought it was beautiful. I liked seeing first-hand what it is like inside, to see where the people pray, where they serve *langar* (vegetarian food served free of charge to all visitors), and to learn what goes on there. It definitely made me fall in love with Sikhism even more, and I was determined to keep learning.

MONEY

When I arrived back home from dropping Abbey off, my mum said, 'I really like that she bought that picture for me.' I think this is what broke down the barrier for her, what made her decide to fight for us. Mum could see Abbey's special personality and why I liked her so much. She knew I would never have thought of doing something like getting that picture, so she could see that Abbey was showing my mum she wasn't going to take me away from my family's culture and religion but was willing to understand it for herself. It was a major breakthrough.

This just left my dad. That was a whole different story, because when my mum started to take it seriously, he got really concerned, and the shouting went on and on. 'No, Money, you cannot do this. It's forbidden. I don't approve,' he'd say, over and over. And he refused to meet Abbey. That took another couple of months. He tried as hard as he could to break us up. He still wouldn't acknowledge she existed, and he said, 'I will disown you if you marry her, Money.' He wanted me to let them find me a girl, but I kept explaining that I was already in love and why would I want them to do that? It was so messed up.

My brother, Ash, who would have been about twelve around then, texted Abbey from my phone one day, pretending to be me, saying I had cheated on her. Then once he knew it had gone through, he deleted it. Abbey just thought it was a weird text. She knew it wasn't me, and when we talked about it, I worked out pretty quickly what had happened. Actually, we thought it was really sweet that Ash cared enough about us as a family that he would think of doing this. There was so much fighting going on and so much hurt, he was trying to keep us apart so all of it would be over.

Later, at the height of the tension, he texted Abbey from his own phone: *'Are you sure you are in love with my brother? Are you going to be good and loyal to him because he is risking his whole family for you?'* It showed how important his family was and how bad things were at home. And once Abbey promised that she loved me, Ash was on her side and never looked back. He was the second one in the family she met. I wanted her to meet at least one person she didn't need to be scared of, so I told Mum and Dad that I was taking Ash to Rainbow's End amusement park for the day. And I warned Ash that if he wanted to go there to shut up and not say anything to our parents about Abbey being with us. We had a great day together and everyone got on but, of course, my parents found out and were furious. 'How could you expose Ash like this?' It was my mum's turn to go off at me again. 'You are confusing him. This is never going to happen between you. Stop doing this nonsense. Stop defying us!'

With my dad so angry, Mum had switched sides, she started listening to him and leaning his way. I understand why she did. She still had to live with him and look after him, whatever else happened. The tension built and built. It had to explode. The final crisis was when they demanded I leave the house.

I broke down in tears. I was heartbroken and exhausted. 'What do you want? What do you expect from me? I've done everything else that you've asked. I'm studying, working, trying to keep up the good reputation in front of everybody. What more do you want?'

Dad had never seen me cry. I had cried in front of my mum, but that was the first time he had witnessed it. It got through to him what this was doing and what Abbey meant, with me refusing to let her go. He saw how much it was affecting me. My parents talked it over at great length and then he finally relented. 'Money, if she is the one, I will meet her and we will get to know her. If she learns to understand our culture, then ... we'll have to see.'

I was allowed to be with Abbey!! I couldn't believe it. Then once they'd given their approval, every other family member knew – immediately. Our parents made sure the word got out because they didn't want us to get caught together somewhere by a relative who didn't know what was going on. That would have been incredibly embarrassing for them.

All this opposition we'd received had a silver lining – it brought Abbey and me so close. I opened up to her a lot over that time, telling her things about my life and she told me about her past. If I'd had a nasty fight at home, I would go straight to Abbey and talk it through with her and she'd calm me down before I went back to the house. Sometimes I'd get home to another argument or there'd be long silences between us, yet, as much as I was fighting for Abbey, she was bringing me closer to my family. Then the decision was made and there was no turning back: our relationship was accepted.

ABBEY

I didn't tell Mum what was going on at this stage, as much as I could have done with her support. My thinking was, if it worked out and I was accepted as Money's partner, I didn't want her to judge the situation or think Money's parents didn't want me in their family. No mother would want that for their child. This way my mum could get to know them on her own terms if she eventually met them. So I was quite vague about it all, just telling her we were having some cultural issues.

It was Ash's birthday when I eventually met Money's dad. Because it was a special occasion, the whole family was going to be there, so I would meet everyone at the same time. They didn't even fit in one room, there were so many of them. I was terrified of doing the wrong thing. I knew to wear a long dress because legs have to be covered – but I didn't wear tights under the dress, so you could still see my calves. Money drove me all the way to his parents' house like that without noticing and I had no idea there was anything wrong.

'Oh no, her legs,' said Pam when she saw me. 'You better drive her home so she can get some tights on and then bring her back.'

I hadn't even walked into the house yet. I was so embarrassed walking in the second time, because everybody knew I'd already made a mistake. Once we were inside, I had to greet all the relatives older than me by going around and touching their feet as a sign of respect. But I didn't expect there'd be at least twenty people to do this to! The idea is you are asking for their blessing and, in return, they put their hand on your head to show they grant you this blessing. There is such respect shown to the elders in Punjabi culture. (Money's cousins who are younger than me touch my feet now, which is so sweet.) So this was how Money's dad and I met. I felt really shy and nervous but I touched his feet and he patted me on the head. We didn't speak much on that occasion but I will never forget what a big deal it was to have got through that and that we were in the same room. Thankfully, there was a little cousin there, Honey, who stayed by my side the whole time and showed me what to do. She's pleased to have another girl she can hang out with because it's nearly all boys in Money's family otherwise. I just did what she did. I was so grateful to her for supporting me. A lot of the time, the males and females are kept separate at these family events, so to know she was there was important as I didn't even have Money to help me on the day.

As I was meeting each person, I wasn't introduced as Money's girlfriend – I was introduced as 'the girl Money wants to marry'. Money had explained that the title of 'boyfriend' and 'girlfriend' is not part of their culture. You only introduce a girl or boy to your family because you are planning to marry them. Everyone was checking me out and staring at me from across the room. I was so scared; I felt I was being judged with each move I made. I was trying to do everything right and be respectful and make a good impression. At one point, Money's mum took me into another room and fed me some *dejh* (a holy food you eat when you attend the *Gurdwara* or it would be prepared for certain events, a bit like getting communion), but she didn't have time to explain what was going on or what it was. 'Eat it, it is good,' she encouraged. She threw a *chunni* (scarf) over my head and thrust some more *dejh* into my mouth.

She was also trying really hard to make sure I did everything right so that no one in the room could say anything like, 'Oh, did you see? She didn't help her mother-in-law serve the food' or whatever else they could take offence at. If I hadn't done the correct things in the correct order, one of them might say, 'See, this is why we don't want people to marry outside of the culture.'

Money didn't think there was anything strange about any of this, it was just normal life for him and he was so happy I was able to meet everyone. But literally every second I was there I was on edge, and my mind was racing about what I should do next and how they were feeling about me and whether I was doing okay. And I wanted to reach out and hold Money's hand or have his arm around me when he came into the room to know he was there and supporting me, but that wouldn't have been proper either. In Punjabi culture, it isn't seen as proper to display your love in public. To this day, Money doesn't show any displays of affection in front of his parents or my mum, even though I'm sure by now they would be totally okay with it.

We left Ash's birthday, and I felt so relieved, I could have sat in the car and cried. But I am actually pleased now it happened this way. If I'd had to meet his relatives individually and repeat that experience over and over again, it would have been worse. This way, I didn't have to talk to everyone because it wasn't possible to, and with so many people there, there was just a lot of watching and learning and smiling and doing what I was told, but all during just one visit. Not long after this, one of Money's uncles took his dad aside. 'It is their future,' he announced, 'we cannot control their lives.' This was what Money's parents needed to hear. It was like they had been given the green light to let this happen. And for Money, this was the moment he knew he could marry me.

MONEY

Once my family had given their approval, so much changed; the difference was incredible. I was able to go on dates with Abbey without sneaking around or hiding the fact. We could go out for dinner – even with Mum and Dad. And they let Abbey sleep over. Not just in the guest room but in *my* room, much to her surprise, especially when Mum brought us a cup of tea in the morning. Although Abbey and I didn't get officially engaged until we'd been dating for about two years, my family had fully accepted her now and even referred to her as the future bride. In our culture, once you are engaged, things are final. There will be no breaking up with this person or seeing someone else. That would not happen. I couldn't come back in three months and say, 'We've broken up. I have a new girlfriend for you to meet.' If I had broken up with Abbey, they would have arranged a marriage for me in India so fast and without any discussion. Saying we're together is as good as being married, so there was no issue about sleeping over at my parents' house – well, not for me, anyway. It took Abbey some time to get used to it.

But they did say no grandchildren yet. That is really all the talk my parents and I had about sex. It just isn't proper in our family to discuss such issues, and because they didn't have a daughter, I have no idea how open they would have been about female matters such as menstruation and so on. But as a male, we didn't talk about anything private or sexual. I couldn't ask, and Dad wouldn't have talked to me. When I got together with Abbey, all Dad said to Mum was, 'Tell him to make sure he doesn't bring a kid into the family before the wedding.'

Having met Abbey, my parents' attitudes and opinions completely turned around. It's funny to hear how they talk about it now. Mum says things like, 'I'm so glad you fought for this. It's one of the best decisions you've ever made. If we'd gone through with an arranged marriage, who knows what that girl would have been like? What if an arranged bride had come in and she wasn't family oriented?' That's the sort of unknown within arranged marriages that is such a risk. My parents may not have realised how much India has changed from when they were growing up. Not as many couples are prepared to go along with the old ways just because it's how it always was. You don't hear much from the Indian community about how hard an unsuitable arranged marriage is for both parties. From when I was thirteen, Mum had been telling me there would be an arranged marriage – but now she cannot ever imagine anyone for me but Abbey. Mum and Dad love Abbey so much. They love the way Abbey brought me back to my family. I was pretty separated from them by the time they met her, and they know how instrumental she's been in bringing us together – which is one of the great ironies, considering they were terrified she would do the complete opposite and split us further apart.

Long before Abbey and I had to fight for our love marriage, my uncle met and fell in love with an Indian girl in New

Zealand and wanted to get married outside the traditional system. He announced this to my father.

'It's not happening,' said Dad. 'You have to go to India, have a bride arranged and bring her back. We can't change our morals and customs because we are in a different country.'

'No. I love her very much and I'm marrying her,' said my uncle.

Nothing happens fast in our family and this argument dragged on for months. One time, my uncle locked himself in his room and wouldn't come out; he wouldn't answer his phone. Dad was knocking on the window from outside, then trying to bust the door open. Everyone started to panic.

Finally, Dad gave in. 'Okay if you want to marry her, you marry her,' he said. And the marriage has worked, just like my uncle predicted it would, because he knew who he was and what he wanted. My uncle's situation played heavily on my mind over the time of our own family fights. I kept thinking, *If my uncle can fight until he gets them to agree, then maybe I can too*. But, just as life is easier for Ash, with me paving the way for his generation to choose what they want to do and when, I know we've made it easier for couples coming along after us. I have a cousin here who is dating someone from a different culture. His family are back in India and now they are not at all concerned. Yes, it is easier because his parents don't actually have to see it all happening in person, but they are so happy he has found someone he loves.

It was such a difficult time for everyone involved, but especially for the two of us. Months and months of stress and arguments and heartache. But we knew what we wanted, we believed in our love and we were prepared to fight to be together. It has made us stronger and closer, and everyone acknowledges this now. They cannot imagine us not being together; they cannot believe what our love has done for our family and for our Punjabi community and at the *Gurdwara*. Everyone loves what our love has shown and they're proud to be part of our journey. Still, we never want to go back there; we're so relieved the whole chapter is behind us.

CHAPTER EIGHT

Detour to Scotland

ABBEY

When I was younger, I used to pine for Scotland but I refused to go back. Partly, I was still annoyed with my dad, partly I was trying to find my own way, but mainly I was scared of how I would feel being back and how hard it would be to go through another goodbye. So I avoided going altogether. Mum offered to send me back when I was fifteen because she could see I was really missing my grandparents especially – but it would be just me going as we couldn't afford for everyone to go. 'It will be a big responsibility, Abbey, going all that way on your own,' she warned.

But I was excited and couldn't wait for the time to come closer. One of Mum's conditions was that Dad had to pick me up from Heathrow Airport in London, but Dad said he couldn't. He said I would have to get to Glasgow and he would collect me there. That meant more flights and more airlines, but he kept saying he had work and other commitments and it was too much to come down to London. Mum said if she was getting me across to the other side of the world, the least he could do is get me the rest of the way to Bellshill. And when he still said it wasn't possible, I didn't feel like I was his priority. Again. I changed my mind and said I didn't want to go back after all.

I do miss Scotland and my extended family and it's hard how far away it is, but I'd say it is more like my second home now; New Zealand is my first. Mum still calls Scotland 'home' and has been back a few times to see her parents, but going that far is really expensive, and once Covid-19 hit, it has been out of the question to travel. Like so many other families dealing with being apart, the separation from Granny is awful and we just wish we could be with her.

I spent my seventeenth birthday alone in New Zealand while Mum was in Scotland. My grandfather's health had taken a turn for the worse and Mum needed to be there. Somehow it happened that on my nineteenth birthday, everyone was over there again, including my brother and sister, so I was without family, but Money came and spent the day with me, which was great. He surprised me with a bottle of my favourite perfume, and a cheeky card that had a camera on the front of it and the words: 'I'm not a photographer, but I can picture us together'. Ha ha. And he signed it from $. We hung out and watched movies and we felt so relaxed. It was rare back then to spend all that time together as his family didn't know about me then.

Returning to Scotland as an adult, and this time bringing Money with me, was so different. I also found myself comparing my childhood town to living in Auckland. I come from quite a religious family and I went to a Catholic primary school, so back then there was exposure to religion on a daily basis. Granny is a staunch Catholic. She says the rosary regularly, and it was usual for me to go to church with her because that is what she likes to do. She's involved in her local parish, helping out and supporting the priest. I was aware of how much of this life we'd let slip in New Zealand. There was no church community in Auckland and we didn't go to church much after we came to New Zealand. As well, Dad isn't Catholic, which may be another reason we left it behind.

What the church does expose in Scotland is the religious prejudice that goes on there and it's probably why, as an adult, I am tolerant of all religions. Like in many small towns, the Catholic and Protestant schools were side by side – and fully segregated; kids would stare each other down or fight, and we were encouraged to not mix or talk to each other. All in the name of religion. The only other thing I remember is a stage performance at primary school in Bellshill when I played the Virgin Mary in the nativity pageant in front of the congregation. I didn't have to say a single word; I just stood there holding the pretend baby. And I nailed it. Granny was so proud of me. But none of this made me a strong believer; mostly I was tagging along because I loved being with my grandmother.

Another difference is how close-knit the Bellshill community is. Everyone stops and talks to each other on the street, and it's pretty usual that your neighbour is your friend. We were so lucky with the neighbourhood we grew up in. If someone moved in next door, they'd quickly get a key to your house, and we looked out for one another. Although people are friendly in New Zealand, it is not to this same level. In some ways I miss that level of community, but in other ways, I don't really mind not having to talk to every person, and everyone knowing everything about me.

MONEY

Abbey has still not been to India, even though she has become so connected to my Punjabi culture. But I was lucky enough to go to Scotland with Abbey in 2017, and to meet her granny who she loves, and to see her grandfather who had dementia and wasn't well. On the way was a stopover in Los Angeles where we stayed with her great-uncle, who is another migrant in this story. He moved there as a teenager with just $50 in his pocket. He worked really hard and is now a successful property owner. It was such a fast-paced city to visit, but where we had once thought it might be fun to live there, we quickly saw it wasn't our scene. Everyone was so tanned and healthy it looked like they had a filter on their lives and we didn't feel we fitted in. I really liked the Scottish sense of community in Bellshill, though. When we were with Abbey's grandmother, it was as if the whole street knew her; people calling out hello wherever we went. In New Zealand, apart from the ones right next door, your neighbours down the street probably don't know who you are.

Abbey had been to the *Gurdwara* with me, so I wanted to go to the Catholic church with her and her granny. At *Gurdwara*, we sit on the floor, but here we sat on seats, men and women sitting together, not apart like in the Sikh religion, and they read their own prayer book if they chose to bring one. For us, we are read to from the *Guru*

Granth Sahib (the holy book) by the *Granthi* (ceremonial leader). Also, we make a donation when we walk in, whereas during mass, volunteers came around during the service and collected the money from the parishioners. For Abbey and me, now that we are married and are parents, we are more conscious of the two cultures' similarities and differences, and we are comfortable celebrating and supporting both. But what connects us is that we both believe in one God. I could be anywhere, and as long as I know I am in God's house, then I know I am praying. I appreciate how my Sikh religion welcomes anyone, no matter what name they put on their belief.

Abbey's granny and her values reminded me a lot of my Indian culture. Even though Abbey's grandfather was very sick and looking after him was a lot of work for her, Granny did not give up on him. Spending time with her made me think about my own grandmother. Because of our domestic structure, my granny doesn't do the cooking – the younger wife usually takes over this role – but Abbey's granny does everything herself. When we were there, she was seventy-seven years old and buying her own groceries and preparing her own meals. Now she is eighty-two and still going strong and doing everything for herself.

I had hatched a plan to propose to Abbey on Valentine's Day at Edinburgh Castle. I thought it would be the perfect romantic setting. I had watched a lot of European movies and knew that when a man is about to propose, he asks permission from the girl's parents, so before we left New Zealand, I rang Abbey's mum.

'Would you like to meet for a coffee?'

'Sure – I'd love to see you,' she said.

'Abbey won't be coming. It will just be us.'

I imagine she knew something was up. And when I asked her permission, she told me she would love me as a son-in-law and how Abbey and I are so perfect for each other. She wanted to know how I was going to propose and I could see her getting emotional when she heard it was to take place in Scotland. I showed her the ring my mother had picked out. In our culture, the mother picks out a ring way before any weddings are organised, and so my mum had already done this for me and my brother. With arranged marriages, the ring doesn't hold the same symbolism as in Western cultures. As the eldest and the first to marry, I chose which of the two rings I would like to give to Abbey, and fortunately, Mum has good taste, so they were both beautiful rings. I had already told my mother about my plan to propose to Abbey and she'd straightaway run inside and opened her box of jewellery for me to select the ring. She'd said, 'Go get her,

Money. You have the family's blessings and nothing will ever come between you.' She was very excited. In her mind it was the right time – after all, it had been two years.

The next step was to talk to Abbey's father when we were in Scotland. This was hard. I had never met Craig but I wanted to do the right thing by Abbey. A few days before Valentine's Day, I asked his permission. He gave me a hug and a dad-like pat on my back and welcomed me to the family. After this, it was just a matter of ensuring I had the ring in my pocket when we left for the castle. We were all set to go. It was going to happen that day.

Then I chickened out.

Edinburgh Castle is such a popular tourist spot and there were so many people around, I lost my nerve. It felt like everyone was on a date and there was romance in the air but it was full-on and didn't seem like the right place or atmosphere after all. Another reason – or maybe it was an excuse – but a couple of days later it was Abbey's grandparents' sixtieth wedding anniversary. I decided this would be the symbol for our own relationship, that we wanted ours to last forever, too. But, unfortunately, Abbey was really sick at her dad's house that day – I had never seen her so sick. To think I could have proposed to her at the romantic, historic setting of Edinburgh Castle, and now it all got a little confusing – but by the end it was funny.

We were lying on the bed, and I turned to her and said, 'If I were to propose to you, would you want like a big proposal?' and she said no, she'd just want it from the heart. So then I said, 'Okay, so if I were to propose to you—' and I casually listed all the things I loved about her. I remember I was literally shaking; I can't believe she didn't pick up on any of this. I was saying, 'You are the most beautiful person I've ever met. I'm so glad we have managed to get through everything we've been through and that we are where we are today.' But Abbey stopped me. She was laughing and saying, 'If you were proposing to me, I would hope you would get down on one knee, hold my hand, look me in the eyes and be all romantic.' She was still fooling around and here I was trying to propose and she didn't realise. So I did all those things. I knelt down and I looked her in the eye, and when I'd finished, I asked if she would marry me. Abbey turned over as if to go back to sleep and was still laughing at me. Seriously. I had to hold the ring out in front of her, and say, 'Abbey, I'm actually proposing to you.' Her mouth opened so wide, and her eyes. I could see she felt bad for not picking up what was going on, but I wasn't making it easy, either. She gave me the biggest hug and said, 'Of course. Yes!' She also loved that it was on her grandparents' wedding anniversary.

Her grandmother's house was just one street over from her father's and as luck would have it, when we looked out the window we saw her walking past, heading home with her shopping. 'Granny, he proposed to me!' Abbey yelled out, and in her grandmother's typical style, she turned and went straight back to the shops and bought a bottle of champagne for us. And when Abbey felt better, we celebrated with everybody.

ABBEY

Our wedding plans brought things to a head with my dad. It was lovely he had been welcoming to Money and was happy to celebrate our news. But when he had been invited to the wedding with plenty of time to plan and book flights – and Money even offering to pay for his flight out if that would help – my father didn't reply to that offer, and eight months before the wedding, he told me he wouldn't be coming because he couldn't afford it. Yet again he had placed other things before me and not made me his priority. This deeply upset me. How could he miss such an important event in my life?

I had had enough. I felt like I had tried to create and nurture a positive relationship between us so many times and never got anywhere. This time I gave up. There were only so many times I would try. Things are not too good even to this day, and we have no contact. I know he is well and he knows I'm well but we don't really talk or know much more about each other. I still love him and have a lot of fond memories. We were very close when I was young, but it hurts that over the years I was the one who had to be strong when they argued, or hug Mum when he left, or console him when he was upset and tell him I was there for him. I don't think that should have been my responsibility. I took the adult burden of trying to fix things onto my young shoulders – and I still have to stop myself from doing this for people today.

I kept trying for a long time. When I look back now, I'm glad the wedding 'crisis' happened because it meant I knew where I stood once and for all. My mum walked me down the aisle and that made me so happy and she deserved that moment. She was the parent who had supported me the whole way through and I loved that she was there to give me away on the day.

CHAPTER NINE

Four Ceremonies and a Riot

MONEY

There is nothing quite like an Indian wedding – or should I say 'weddings', because in our case we had four ceremonies, the last resulting in a brawl where the police had to be called.

In India, the two families' parents usually split the costs 50/50 as the weddings are so large, but because we were having separate occasions, my parents paid for the Indian ceremonies and Abbey's mum paid for the European one. I didn't know what would be expected of us. My mum made the decisions for the Indian events because Abbey had no idea what traditions had to be included and how to plan for such an event, and I didn't know either. With our European wedding, it was different. We planned it. Actually, Abbey planned it, and every now and then she would ask my opinion. Usually I would be given two options and I always prayed that the one I chose was the one I was meant to choose.

'What colour for the flowers, do you think? This or that?'

'Umm – this one.'

'Are you sure?'

'Umm – maybe that one.'

'Oh, sweet, I agree, we'll go with that colour.'

I learnt a lot while planning our European wedding. This is not something I ever expected I would be doing in my life. Also, there were so many minor details we had to think about. If Abbey hadn't taken charge, we would probably still not be married. I was responsible for three main tasks on the day (apart from being the groom). I had to show up wearing the correct clothes, make sure to bring the cake to the venue, and put out signs we'd made that said 'Don't take a side, take a seat.' This was a small gesture we wanted to make right up front. We didn't want the two families as they walked in to immediately sit on separate sides; we wanted everyone to mix and mingle.

I got to the wedding venue an hour early because I was so stressed about ensuring everything went okay. Then someone asked, 'Where is the cake? I can't wait to see it.' Oh my God. I didn't have the cake. And it was a 30-minute drive each way to get it. I was saved by the florist offering to go instead. No one told Abbey until much later. We had also planned for the ceremony to be held out in the venue's lovely garden setting, but the day arrived and it was typical Auckland weather – warm but pouring with rain – so we had to pack up the chairs and have it inside instead. Not long ago, Abbey told me I also forgot about bringing the sign – and all my side of the family were on one side, and hers on the other. Really? I couldn't believe it.

But I *was* dressed in the right suit.

My extended family had only seen European weddings in movies so they were excited to be here and part of it – and for me, it was unbelievable to think I'd reached this milestone where I could marry Abbey in this setting with my family there witnessing it and supporting us. What a long and difficult road to get here.

We wanted to incorporate aspects of both cultures into the ceremony. One Scottish wedding tradition is that the two mothers bring a piece of fabric from their respective cultures – my mum carried an Indian-patterned material and Abbey's mum a Scottish one. They tied our wrists together with the material, to symbolise bringing our cultures together. Abbey's mum made sure there was a bagpiper out the front to welcome all the guests and pipe them in. And my dad had made me a waistcoat out of Scottish tartan, which was such a beautiful gesture and I wore it very proudly.

I stood up at the altar waiting for Abbey and when she walked down the aisle towards me, with her mum by her side, honestly, Abbey was just breathtaking. She looked like an angel, all in white. My dreams had come true. I loved the chance to declare my love for Abbey in the traditional wedding vows – another custom I'd only ever seen done in films. We both thought a lot about what we wanted to say to each other. In some of my lines, I said: 'Abbey, you're the biggest blessing I could have ever asked for, you complete me. You are the one who makes me chuckle when I'm miserable, the one who makes me stop and think when I want to be impulsive, and the person who brings me down to reality when I'm sky high. Today, standing here in front of our family and friends, I promise to spend the rest of my life adoring you and respecting you. As I've given you my hand to hold, so I give you my life to keep.'

Abbey's vows were incredible and I love that we have them to look back on and remember. Some of her lines were: 'When we were asked to list what we loved about the other person, mine honestly became too long to list. Everything from your adorable chin dimple, your amazing jawline, beautiful eyes, and long thick eyelashes that I'm so jealous of as you don't even need them, to your humour and your loving heart. I really scored the jackpot with you and consider myself the luckiest girl to be marrying you today … I vow to be your best friend and wife forever, and your ride or die. *Mein tenu pryaar karde a jaan* ("I love you my life" in Punjabi), I love you forever and always.'

I worried about having to kiss Abbey in front of my family. This is something we would never do in our ceremonies – or anywhere. I have never seen my parents kiss and I have seen them hug only once. I knew it was usual to kiss Abbey at the wedding, and I wanted to, but I still felt awkward. When it came time for the 'you may now kiss the bride' moment, I did, then looked back nervously – to see my relatives clapping and cheering! It was just like they had seen in the movies. I even had my first glass of champagne when we were doing the toasts.

We spent a lot of time worrying whether everyone else was having a good time, and there was so much talking and meeting people who wanted to congratulate us at the reception, but Abbey and I made sure we slipped away for little breaks, just the two of us. It was so romantic and I felt like my heart would burst, I was so happy. And everyone loved the day. One of my relatives came up to me and said, 'Money, this is one of best weddings I have been to. I am so glad I got to see a European wedding in my lifetime.'

That meant a lot. Deciding on the guest list had actually been a real issue because we couldn't have the same numbers of guests at each event. At an Indian wedding there is no limit to the numbers, and if someone is invited, they can bring along anyone else they choose. This is how my Indian relatives understood things went, but at the European wedding venue, it catered for 100 people in total, and so for me to have to say that many of them would miss out as we each only had fifty close family members we could invite was very tricky.

Another tradition, of going on a honeymoon straight after our wedding, couldn't happen because we had the whole set of Punjabi wedding celebrations the following week to get ready for, and 200 people attending each event. These had taken such a huge amount of planning and preparation for my mum. First of all, my parents had to find a *Gurdwara* that was free on the date. There aren't many in Auckland so they thought it would be straightforward and easy enough, however, they immediately encountered prejudice at the first temple where they were told they wouldn't allow it to take place there. It was an interesting turnaround for Mum, who had not approved of a mixed marriage and now she was on the receiving end of prejudice – and she was outraged. It was also shocking to be refused because the Sikh religion is about being open and welcoming to everyone. But the temple in

Papatoetoe, *Gurdwara* Sri Dasmesh Darbar, agreed to host the wedding, so our planning got underway.

The first of the Indian ceremonies is *Mahiyan* (also called *Vatna*), which is a cleansing ceremony. Every ritual performed during a Sikh wedding is significant. *Mahiyan* takes place in the morning about three days before the wedding. Ours was held in a tent at my parents' house, where a thick paste was rubbed over our face, arms and feet. The key ingredient, turmeric, is used for various reasons: the spice is supposed to brighten the skin, it brings good luck, it helps calm and ease the nerves, while some say *Mahiyan* is about letting everyone have some fun before the big day. The paste at our *Mahiyan* was mixed with yoghurt. I had already warned Abbey about this, but poor Abbey – she hates yoghurt, even the smell of it.

The second event is *Jaggo*, which is a big party two nights before the official Sikh wedding, the *Anand Karaj*. Our *Jaggo* was held at a venue in Manukau. It is for all the guests to have the time of their lives, dancing and singing and using up lots of energy before the marriage itself. My mum's family was responsible for this event. It was another occasion where I was so pleased that some of them now live in New Zealand or were here visiting because there were so many traditions to it and it was really good to have them guiding us. Traditionally, at the *Jaggo*, which literally means 'wake up', the groom and his family would take a pot with candles in it from house to house in their Indian village as a way of inviting people to the wedding. They'd say, 'My son is getting married. Would you add some oil to the pot to make the candles last longer? And come to the wedding.' We didn't have a village to make our way around, but we still had the candles, even if they were fake ones, and we all danced outside and chanted and yelled and took turns holding the pot on our heads. It was brilliant fun.

As well as all the preparations, my parents had picked out the outfits we would wear. They'd showed Abbey a few designs first, to make sure she liked what they were thinking, and then they ordered everything from India. They travelled there a few months before, with a long list of everything to buy: jewellery, clothes and shoes for everyone. There are shops in Auckland that can supply these things, but it was more economical to go to India, get everything there and bring it back. And there was a lot to buy. It wasn't just the outfits. The groom's mum and dad have to give the bride's family gifts, traditionally this is gold and blankets to symbolise financial security and warmth. Because Abbey didn't have many relatives, my mum also gave my aunties and uncles a ring and a blanket. It was important to follow these customs so my parents were seen to be fulfilling their obligations.

I cannot get over how incredible Abbey was during this whole time and how grateful I am she just went with the flow. There was so much she had to deal with and put up with and learn on the spot. She never once said 'I need this', or 'No, sorry, I'm not going to do that.' She trusted the choices that were being made for her and she just accepted everything and played her part in such a gracious way. And she made the most beautiful bride.

ABBEY

Money and I obviously weren't seeing each other for the first time like they do with arranged marriages, but we still chose to keep apart before the ceremonies. Money's uncle lives in the house behind his parents, and so my family and I stayed there. Something similar had happened the week before at the European wedding, where my mum rented a cottage near the venue and all of the women in our family came and spent the night with me and we had a brilliant 'final girls' night' before I got married.

For the Indian ceremonies, we were totally relying on Money's parents to tell us every step of the way what to do and what part of the proceedings was coming up. On the morning of the *Jaggo*, they hired a company that applies henna. My sister and sister-in-law (our brother's wife) joined me for this at the uncle's house. I had to sit still for five hours while my arms and legs were decorated and painted, then I rubbed lemon juice and sugar over it when the design was finished. You could see the henna designs at the *Jaggo* that evening, and already they looked amazing. The next morning, mustard oil was rubbed into it to enhance the colour – it's the heat from the oil that deepens the shade – and I loved how it turned out. It lasts for quite a while, which was one reason for having the European wedding first.

On the morning of our 'second' wedding, our *Anand Karaj*, after already days and days of events and people, I was told I needed to be up and showered to start preparing at four o'clock in the morning. No joke. And as if this wasn't bad enough, some of the women in Money's family came in and started throwing yoghurt over me and rubbing it into my face and hair – which the hairdresser had specifically said not to wash on the morning of the wedding – and now I absolutely needed to. I can't remember what that ritual symbolised. I was just so shocked and they were all laughing and yelling. The woman doing my makeup and hair started at five o'clock and was still going at ten, when I was supposed to be arriving at the *Gurdwara*. I was so late. But everyone else kept interrupting her, asking her to fix them and sort them out, and I could tell she was getting more and more annoyed.

The usual way to start the proceedings of the wedding ceremony is the *milni*. It's like a formal introduction of the members of both families, and garlands are exchanged, but because my family was so small in comparison to Money's, the *Granthi* did a welcoming/opening ceremony outside the *Gurdwara* with just them, the groom's side, while my family stood inside the door. Then, in another custom, which is supposed to be like a bargain to see if he is allowed in to marry me, the females in my family held a ribbon across the doorway. Money had brought gifts for them, and in return, they bartered and fed him sweets, until they handed him the scissors to cut the ribbon and enter the *Gurdwara*.

Everyone was then served breakfast in the hall until it was time for the *Anand Karaj*, which means 'blissful union', to begin. All the guests headed into the *darbar* (main hall) where they bowed to the holy book, the *Guru Granth Sahib*. Money then entered, escorted in by his brother, brother-in-law, his mum and her sister-in-law. Then it was my turn. My brother and sister walked with me, as well as my sister-in-law and cousins. I felt incredible in my beautiful red *lengha* (full-length skirt), but inside I was a bundle of nerves. I kept focusing only on Money, and his handsome face, knowing I could get through this, even if I had no idea what I was doing from one minute to the next.

The *Granthi* read from the holy book, and then, instead of signing the marriage register as we do at a European ceremony, we had to walk around the holy book four times, slowly, together, each holding one end of a piece of cloth. There hadn't been a rehearsal so everyone just did what they were told. At another stage, my brother and sister had to sit in opposite corners and 'pass' me from one to the other and then to Money, which symbolises my family letting me go. In a Sikh wedding, the equivalent of a European best man is more like a 'best child' because it is a younger male relative who fills this role. Following this tradition, Money was his uncle's best man when he got married and Ash was Money's at our wedding. It is amazing to think that our son, Noah, will be Ash's best man when the time comes. That is how the circle continues.

Traditionally, when the couple leaves the temple as husband and wife, the bride is handed rice. I was told to throw it behind me to my family to catch, a symbolic way of saying 'Thank you for all the food you have given me. Here is my love back to you.' I was also supposed to be upset, because the custom is that the wife is leaving her family to live with her husband's family, but in our case, I wasn't crying, I was just so happy. Money's relatives thought this was very cute because I was saying, 'Why would I be sad? I'm marrying the man of my dreams.'

There were many rituals we couldn't follow that would happen in an Indian village – such as someone producing a horse and an elephant – but we covered a lot of them.

Money with his mum, when he was around a year old, at a family wedding. Funny fact: He somehow lost his pants that night!

Money and his mum on the day they left for New Zealand, in 1998, with Money's father's parents. Money's grandmother lives near us now. Noah is named after his great-grandfather: Inder is one of his middle names.

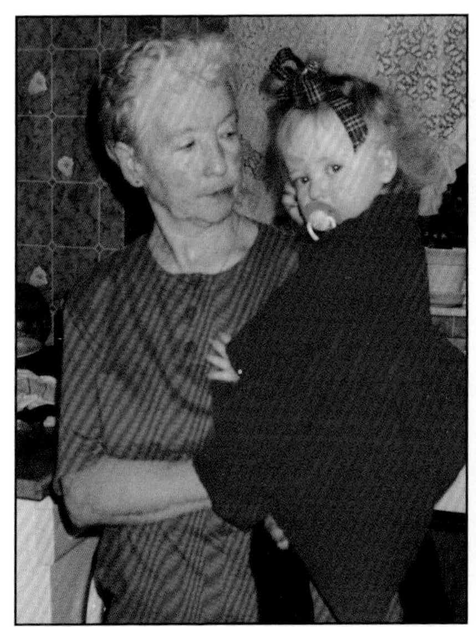

Abbey, 18 months old, with her granny on Christmas Day, 1997. Under her coat, Abbey is wearing a traditional tartan dress that matches the bow in her hair.

The love between Abbey and her grandpa, William, was undeniable. She is two and a half here. Noah is also named after him: William is another of his middle names.

Money, around six or seven years old, with his parents in New Zealand. This is one of the few family photos where Money is still wearing a *patka*.

Abbey (left) on her first day of school in Scotland, with her best friend, Lizzie. Abbey and Lizzie are still in touch – the friendship has definitely lasted!

At Money's citizenship ceremony, in 2003, with his parents and Ash, then a toddler. Money had a camera and was vlogging and taking photos the whole day – he knew what his career would be all along, ha ha.

Abbey at her performing arts school.

Money before a shift at The Warehouse, with his arm around his dad. He was 18 then and so excited to have a car, passed down from his father.

One of our first dates, at the Sky Tower. Money had surprised me by buying and installing a new stereo in my car, and I took him to a nice dinner as a thankyou.

The photo below was taken about a year into our relationship, after Money's family knew about us. We were attending a family friend's wedding and Money's mum got me ready; she did my hair and chose my outfit, which I thought was super sweet.

Out at a nightclub with friends, before our families knew about us and when we were still getting to know each other.

Money's father and mother on their wedding day, in 1992. As they were in a traditional arranged marriage, this was only the fourth time they had seen one another.

Celebrating with Money's parents on their wedding anniversary. In Money's family, it's a tradition to feed cake to someone celebrating a special occasion, so I fed both of his parents.

During our trip to Scotland. On Valentine's Day, we went out to dinner with Abbey's father and his girlfriend. We had such a nice time together.

Money proposed to me in Scotland, and we decided to have our official engagement photoshoot after we returned to New Zealand. We spent a beautiful day remembering the proposal and just being so in love with one another!

With Money's mum, attending a family friend's *Anand Karaj* (Indian wedding). The day was very special, and I got to meet so many of the extended family.

Attending a cousin's *Jaggo*, about 10 months before we were married. This night was so much fun, and I got to experience the celebration from a close, family perspective and see everything that would happen during our upcoming event.

With Money's mum on Mother's Day, before Money and I were married. After a long shift, working until 8 pm, I surprised her with some flowers and goodies before going home and doing the same for my mum.

The day Money's mum's relatives arrived for our wedding. Money's *Mama-ji* is in the centre, wearing the pink turban. We were all so excited to pick them up from the airport and spend as much time with them as we could.

At our European wedding. We allocated time at the end of the evening for just the two of us. This was the last photo taken of us as newly married husband and wife, right before we slipped away and left for the night.

With Abbey's stepfather, Mike, and her mum.

At the wedding reception, Abbey's mum had a song performed that describes how she feels about us. I got so emotional hearing it, and we gave her a massive hug.

During the *Mahiyn* (*Vatna*), the first of our Indian wedding events, we were covered with a turmeric and yoghurt paste. This ritual is performed to cleanse and purify you before your big day.

Abbey at our *Jaggo* – the second Indian wedding event, traditionally held the night before the *Anand Karaj*. The couple goes around with a *jaggo* – a vessel containing oil and lit candles – on their heads. People fill the *jaggo* with more oil to symbolise that they accept your invitation to the wedding. The event carries on long into the night, with much dancing and singing.

Our *Anand Karaj*. After our Indian wedding ceremony, held at the *Gurdwara*, we went to Cornwall Park for photos and then everyone went to Money's parents' house for a full day of games and rituals.

At our Indian wedding reception. After this final event, we stayed at Money's parents' for the night, as is customary, and followed further traditions the next morning.

Our first *Lohri* celebration as a married couple, although it wasn't our own. Only a month or so after our wedding.

Abbey's graduation from university. She graduated with a Bachelor of Arts degree, majoring in psychology and with a minor in criminology. We didn't know it at the time, but Abbey was already pregnant with Noah by then.

A picture taken during our pregnancy with Noah, only a few weeks before he arrived.

Noah's first Christmas, right after we moved into our new home. Noah wore a different festive outfit for each of the 12 days of Christmas.

Noah's first *Lohri*, in January 2021. The event was so beautiful, celebrating our little munchkin, and he had so much fun dancing and singing with everyone.

All of us in matching traditional Punjabi attire. Money's parents brought these suits back from India for us when I was still pregnant with Noah. It was fun to be finally wearing them.

Announcing our second baby, due March 2022. Little Miss Mini Singh, we are so excited to meet you!

Money even had a sword that he carried with him the whole day. Without being able to describe everything in detail, I do remember we had to play these games that act out some old traditions. In one, the sisters-in-law must get together and demand money from the groom or they won't let him have his bride. Then they stole Money's shoes, for him to pretend to pay to get them back. There's another called 'fish the ring'. The ring is in a bowl of milk, with rose petals and rice and things to make it harder to find, and we literally had to fight with our hands and be the first to grab the ring. The idea is whoever gets the ring, over the three times we try, is said to be the boss of the relationship. Everyone was laughing so hard and all of Money's family were on my side to win the game. One popular ritual – by this time we were at Money's family house – is called *God Baithai*, where the brother of the groom must sit on the bride's lap, except in our case it was all of Money's male cousins. It was so hilarious because there are a lot of them. This game is a joking way of showing that I am becoming a mother figure, I am now their *bhabi*, which is why they each sit on my lap. And I give them money to show my love and that I will always be there for them.

I can't even tell you how huge these days were. I remember feeling anxious and scared most of the time that I was going to mess up somehow or embarrass myself, and it was good to know that Money also felt pretty scared and nervous. And yet I was also super excited as it meant I was becoming part of Money's future, his life, his family and his culture. It was beautiful for me to experience and learn about the different traditions but it was pretty overwhelming. At the end of each of these long days, I needed some alone time to recharge, to prepare for the next one. I was still a very shy, reserved person back then and wasn't used to being around so many people, so it was a lot to get used to, but I can genuinely say I really did enjoy it.

The last celebration at an Indian wedding is just one huge party. It was all going well and everyone was dancing and having a good time, but near the end of the night, a riot started, with furniture being thrown and people carted off by the police. Apparently this is very common at Indian weddings, but no one thought to tell me! It will probably always be unclear as to how it properly began, but we know that one of Money's friends, who was pretty drunk by then, decided to bring a bottle of champagne onto the dance floor. Then he shook the bottle, intending to spray it everywhere – like some Formula 1 race – but not ideal at a wedding.

One of the security guards at the venue immediately came up to him. 'Sorry, mate – there's no alcohol allowed on the dance floor. Safety reasons.'

'What are you going to do about it?' the guy snarled.

'I'm going to take that bottle away,' said the security guard, and ripped it out of his hands.

Who knows why, but it all turned manic. Money's friend threw a punch, the guard pushed back and suddenly everyone was pouring onto the dance floor throwing fists around. At my wedding. One of their friends, dressed in a black suit, was punched because someone thought he was another security guard, then that guy's whole family came running in. Then Money's aunties, uncles, cousins and friends joined in. It turned into a riot so fast. There were pregnant women in the middle of the fight, men throwing chairs over their heads, children running around yelling, babies crying. Money was in there somewhere as well.

Some genius from the venue turned off all the lights – and that just made it worse because no one stopped throwing chairs, they just couldn't see where they were throwing them. I was screaming at people to calm down, but no one was listening. Or they would stop for a moment to assure me everything was okay, then the moment my back was turned they would start brawling again. My European relatives and friends were huddled at the back of the hall, wondering what the hell was going on. Obviously nobody had told them either that this was a very common way for a Punjabi wedding to end. And because they hadn't seen what started the fight, it made the whole thing even more frightening.

I started bawling my eyes out. My beautiful wedding was being ruined. My sister and my mum were upset too, while others were finding it funny that we were crouched in a corner crying. Even the DJ came over at one point and assured me, 'This happens at every wedding I do. At least this one is in New Zealand. If it were in India, there might have been a gun fired in the air by now. We are used to these escalating from one to 100 in record time.'

Money's parents tried to take care of me. 'You should get out of here,' said Pam. 'You will get hit.' She was holding one of my hands, Money's dad was holding the other and they were trying to get me away.

'No, I need to find Money,' I cried. Now I was fighting his mum. 'Let me go. I'm fine. I need to find Money.'

I ran outside and around to the front of the building as half the fight had spilled out there now. My mum was pulling people out of the brawl by their shoulders or necks – including one of Money's uncles. This uncle doesn't say much; although his English is good, he doesn't think it is, so he avoids talking, which is a bit intimidating as he can have this sullen stance about him, but he is actually lovely. Mum had always mistaken his shyness for him not liking her. Anyway, when she realised it was him she was grabbing, she was terrified, but he thanked her for trying to calm things down. After that night, he and my mum get on really well and he jokes about her dragging him out of the fight.

The whole thing was so frightening. Why didn't anyone warn me this was likely to happen? Then the police arrived to break it up. Money eventually came and found me and saw we needed to get out of there, so we took off.

And that's how our wedding reception ended.

But, no, it wasn't really the end; I'm not sure by then it was *ever* going to be the end, because there were more traditions we were supposed to follow that night. The new wife has to go to the husband's family home to spend the night there, but after all that had just happened, I didn't feel like I could face them. Money and I drove around for a while, catching our breath and me crying and us trying to decide what to do. It wasn't that I didn't want to go there, I just was struggling with my emotions and how much had happened in such a short amount of time.

'If we don't go to my parents' house tonight, we will have to go tomorrow night and make up with them then,' said Money. 'It's so late. Let's go back there and we can sleep.'

It was around one in the morning by this stage and I was so strung out, but then Money's mum called and told us to please come over and they were all fine and to not let it ruin the beautiful events that had happened all week. Many of the guests from the wedding were at the house and waiting for us. So, even though it was so late, we got there and stayed up for ages, talking about the crazy way things had got out of hand. We ended up laughing heaps about it. Money's mum was telling everyone how I fought her off and that she was so proud and it showed again how much I love her son. Some relatives were saying this brawl meant someone had wished bad fortune on us and the fight had undone it, the negativity had been destroyed and there were only positive vibes. So we all thanked God that it had happened.

Was this the last of the games? No. It was time for bed but they had set up the bedroom with roses everywhere and beautiful bed linen. I felt so awkward. We had gone from no one talking about sex, even though I was allowed to stay at their house, to now being told to 'have fun' and 'here, drink this milk'. We had to share a cup of warm milk, which apparently means: 'Drink it together and your love will increase.' Then Money went for a shower and I got into pyjamas and was just in the bedroom talking to Money's mum when she brought over a *chunni* and said I should put it over my head and cover my face. Money was supposed to lift it off when he came into bed, like this grand romantic gesture – how it is done in Bollywood movies on the wedding night for dramatic effect. His mum was taking it so seriously but I kept laughing. Then Money came in, and his mum was prompting him to take the *chunni* off me, but we found it hilarious, even his mum was laughing by then. The three of us sat and talked for a while until I was just too exhausted and had to sleep.

As the new bride, I was still required to make sweets first thing in the morning for all the family who would be arriving to give us presents and money. But for now, I could finally say I was married to Money. Our new life together as husband and wife could begin. There surely would be no more dramas.

CHAPTER TEN

Going Viral

MONEY

We were conscious of wanting to include as many people as possible in our wedding ceremonies, but there were still a lot of people left out. Nearly all my family on my father's side live in New Zealand, and about seven of mum's relatives had made the journey out from India for the occasion, which was an amazing effort and brilliant for Abbey to meet them. But Abbey's grandmother and other friends and family in Scotland couldn't make the trip, and plenty of people living in New Zealand wanted to be part of the occasion as well and couldn't.

Family members had asked me for a copy of the wedding video but I decided it would be better if I just uploaded it to YouTube and anyone who wanted could watch it. It was supposed to be just for our family – but Abbey reckons we underestimated the enthusiasm out there for the traditional Punjabi wedding. Watching a wedding on YouTube is quite a usual thing to do in India. But, this one was a Sikh man, originally from Punjab, marrying a Scottish woman wearing a full Punjabi *lengha*, and both families were obviously fully accepting of this interracial wedding, so maybe we shouldn't have been surprised how quickly it went viral. But it was so unexpected. I didn't even think about whether I should upload it as 'public' or not because it didn't worry us if anyone else chose to view it. Before we knew it, our wedding video was on this social media trending cycle where people start commenting, then more people watched it – and it just went nuts. That was when I organised it better, deleting the twelve separate clips and uploading them again in full clips. They were titled, 'Anand Karaj | Punjabi Wedding | Modern Singhs', and so on, for each one of the events.

Just for fun, and because so many people were commenting and asking to see more from us, we made a video of Abbey reading some of the comments we'd received about our wedding. She was trying to read them aloud in Punjabi or work out what the messages meant. It was really fun to video. We were just being ourselves and laughing and we weren't acting up for the camera, but we really wanted to find a way to reach out to all these people we didn't know who had said such lovely things to us. The reaction was huge. When we started to gain followers with our first wedding videos, we were shocked that people were interested at all. We felt like saying, 'We're not that interesting', but it took off regardless.

We had to work out what to do with this. We weren't sure about getting involved in social media. Do we want to do this? Should we do it? We went back and forth a lot. Then once we decided to give this online presence a go, we needed to choose a name for our channel. This sounds like a simple decision, but there were many angles to consider. We thought of calling it 'The Singh Family' or 'The Singhs' but both names were taken. We tried 'Money and Abbey' but it didn't sound right. We thought of 'The Scindians' – Scottish Indians – but you can hear how bad that sounds. 'The New Zealand Singhs'. 'The New Zealand Indians' … We couldn't seem to find a name that just suited us and said what we wanted it to. When we uploaded the first videos, Abbey had used 'The Modern Singhs', and once we heard it a few times it felt friendly and just right. I talked to my mum to get her perspective and how it might be perceived in our Indian community. She thought it would be okay.

A lot of people ask, 'What's modern about you? You have cut your hair and you've shaved. You've married outside your religion. Is that modern?' They wonder if we might be like others who have left their culture behind and are not celebrating festivals or speaking the language, but on our channel, we do all of that. We are trying to bring a new generation to embrace their culture and roots, while making sure what we show the outside world matches what we are like on the inside.

Singh is our name, but the issue is it is also our religious name. And when we wrote 'modern' in front of it, we didn't want to appear like we were trying to change the religion. Abbey especially didn't want people to think we were saying Sikh religion should change because she comes from outside the religion. It was so important to us that nothing we were doing with our online presence would disrespect the faith or the culture. Honestly, we went over this many times, but nothing else sounded as right as this name. 'You know what?' we said, 'Let's just upload a video with this name and see how it goes.'

So on to YouTube the name went with a video, and I made a Facebook page and we asked all our friends to like it.

Straight afterwards, I remember one of my devout Sikh friends messaged me: 'What is this?' he asked.

'Oh no, we shouldn't have done it,' was my first reaction. I was so scared we were doing something wrong. 'We are changing the name!' I told Abbey.

'We can't change it because of one person's opinion,' she said. My family also reassured me that what we were doing was fine, so I messaged him a couple of days later and explained the channel was about us putting family wedding stuff online. He didn't say anything after that, so I guess he got it. And that friend follows us now; he just wanted to know we were not trying to change the culture.

It was a stressful time for us. If we made a mistake or said the wrong thing in a video, we knew there would be many people who would be quick to call us out on it. This can be really hard to take and be intimidating. But on the other hand, when a devout Sikh who shares our values messages us to say they love us and they love what we are doing, it really fills our hearts with joy and we know that what we have been trying to get across is working. And that is why we've kept doing the videos. At first we couldn't decide, but then we started getting so many comments like 'your videos are helping me so much'; 'you help me appreciate my culture more and it makes me want to wear my traditional clothing in public'. That was one group. Another big section of comments would be responses such as 'you have opened my parents' minds to how it can work if I marry outside my religion'; 'thank you for sharing. My family are more accepting of my decision'.

We had to do a lot of learning, seeing we weren't YouTube people before this. We still aren't, really. We have made connections with other YouTubers since we started. Most of them have a manager or someone to help them, like an editor, but we do it ourselves. From the beginning, we did all our own editing and shooting and uploading – we still feel very rooky, really entry-level. We are all about having fun and that seems to be part of our appeal. We laugh heaps while we show us doing normal things, playing pranks, hanging with Noah, just everyday stuff. We're not trying to be all flash and glossy, our clips don't have these nice transitions and fancy editing, but ours are authentic and that is important to us.

CHAPTER ELEVEN

Our New Relationship

ABBEY

There is much more to being in a relationship than just falling in love and having a beautiful wedding. And we still have a lot to learn – a relationship never stops being something both have to work at. Ours developed into something serious, very quickly. I'm not someone who would normally rush into talking about children on a first date, for example, but it showed me that I had found my person. We had only been together two years by the time Money proposed, which still didn't feel like that long to me. I have friends who have been with their boyfriends for years and are not close to getting married. Yes, Money and I were in love and we saw a future together, but I would not have assumed we would get married yet – which is why I started laughing and joking around at his proposal.

Although it took months for Money to tell his mum and then for his family to be okay about us, once we'd got over that major hurdle, things went crazy. I was in the family then and that was all there was to it. I was treated like his wife from day one, even though we were just dating. It was totally next level. Pam started referring to me as 'Money's future wife' from then on. I remember she would bring relatives into The Warehouse and introduce me as her daughter-in-law, not his girlfriend. And from the beginning, Pam started teaching me how to be a good wife for her son, in ways that were traditionally Punjabi. I really appreciated all her help and guidance on this; I wanted to learn as much as I could. She taught me how to cook Money's favourite Indian foods – well, some of them. Money loves so much of her cooking, but I learnt how to make *shahi paneer* (Indian cheese cooked with cream, tomatoes and spices), *saag* (spiced spinach curry), *kheer* (sweet rice dessert) and other dishes. She showed me how to wear Punjabi suits and a *lengha* correctly, and how to take care of Money the way she did for his father.

Anyone in a relationship knows that there are adjustments and compromises to make. Money and I are no different.

Money didn't like that I wasn't very tidy. He used to get so irritated about the state of my room or my car when we were going out. It drove him nuts. I struggled with the fact that he wasn't the best communicator. He is a lot better now (and I am a lot tidier), but I found this very hard at the start. I am someone who needs to tell the other person exactly how I am feeling and work through these feelings, especially if there is a problem to be sorted out. But if we were having difficulty explaining our points of view, I would try to express how I felt and Money would take it as an insult to him or his culture or his family. Money's family has a habit of talking over each other, no one listens very well, and they just yell and get louder. I am the mediator among them, so maybe I shouldn't have been surprised that Money didn't like to discuss things or would get defensive.

What was good was that Money didn't come into our relationship expecting me to stay home and be a housewife and clean and cook just because I was the female. He encouraged me to study, work and do plenty of things outside of the home. A lot of girls message me online saying they're facing obstacles with this and are dealing with situations such as husbands who are controlling and who don't want them to do things for themselves. Some of this is changing over time, which is really good, but I hope every society is learning to break away from the old rules that keep males and females in their stereotypical roles, especially if someone is feeling trapped and restricted because of it. Anyway, Money has always been a clean freak. He is not hyper OCD, but he likes things in certain ways and cannot handle it if they aren't. For instance, if he is watching TV, the remote has to be lying perfectly straight on the table, otherwise he can't focus on the program. So I've had to help him relax and I also do what I can to ensure order and cleanliness in the house.

Money comes from an extremely diligent family that never stops working. He admits he has a hard time sitting still. If I put on a movie, only twenty minutes into it he will be up cleaning the kitchen bench or vacuuming in another room. Relaxing is not hardwired in his brain. His family is the same, especially Sukhi *Chacha-ji* (typical nickname for your father's younger brother). He works 24/7 – but that is why the whole family has been able to come here from India. Hard work is the only thing that has made that possible. My attitude is that I appreciate hard work and will put in the effort when needed, but I also know it's good to relax and take things easy at times. I have taught Money to relax more, and he has taught me to relax a bit less.

I would never have a clean and tidy room without him around. We even each other out. Now, he will notice the finger marks on the table, but he might not do anything about them until the movie is over. My mum is not the tidiest person either and she always asks how our house can be so clean when we have a one-year-old. She is scared to make a mess when she eats at our place. She knows that as soon as she leaves, the first thing Money does is vacuum up the crumbs. When I was living at my own house, I made my bed by just covering it over with a duvet. That's not how it is done as far as Money is concerned. He has to fluff up the pillows and put the sheets back on properly and pull everything in tight and make it look perfect. It is the little differences like this that make him feel okay. We don't fight about those things now. If I don't do them, he does them.

I never had any doubts about us at the start and I never will. We love each other so much and we have heaps of fun and love being in each other's company. We're just concentrating on making our relationship as solid as possible. Every day. And even though I've been concentrating on how we learnt to work things out, which is an important way to start in a relationship, after we got married it was honestly just pure wedded bliss – finally being able to live together, permanently. For the first month or so, Money's relatives from India were still here, so we got to spend a lot of time with them as everyone wanted to make the most of this. And then not long after that my grandmother came out from Scotland. That was just amazing.

Money and I were still both working at this point and I was still studying then, too, so it was a really busy period. But when we had time off, we had the best time. We were always off on dinner dates, or having friends over for dinner – it was so nice to have our own place to invite friends to – we felt so grown up and adult. We had Money's family or mine over pretty much every day, otherwise we were at theirs. And I remember I wore my *churha*, my red wedding bangles, for three months after the marriage, and people were always stopping us when we were out to congratulate us as they knew what the bangles represented. It was just the happiest time ever!

A few months later we went to Bali for our honeymoon. What a beautiful place. We thought it was such a magical spot – except that Money was absolutely terrified of the lizards, and I would have to always check in the bathroom and the shower that there weren't any on the ceiling before he went in. It made me laugh that it was me being so brave.

Unfortunately, we had no luggage with us for the first three days – our bags had been mislaid somewhere in transit. We were so keen to get into our clean summer clothes by the time we finally saw the luggage sitting there in our room. The other exciting thing about our honeymoon was that by then I was pregnant with Noah. So even though I was extremely sensitive to every strong smell or fast drive on windy roads or, sometimes, I needed to not do anything but lie down, it was a very special time in our lives and we'll always have fond feelings for Bali.

It's important to recognise that relationships aren't always sunshine and holidays. Our worst-ever conflict came down to a lack of communication. It happened when I was pregnant with Noah. The idea around arranged marriages in Indian culture where a woman leaves her home and lives with her in-laws when she gets married was not something we were going to follow. It was an option, but I took a stand on it. We live a five-minute walk away from Money's parents and I am so happy with that, but I couldn't live in the same house. At first his mum wanted us to move in, but eventually Money saw my point of view, and we have our own home. The great thing is that Money's mum now agrees and says we are much closer as family members because we give each other space. It means we are able to have our own relationships in the privacy of our own homes, and then be together and spend quality time at each other's places, for visits.

So, we'd got through that, but then what brought *heaps* of confusion was what happens after a baby is born. In Punjabi families, it is usual that for forty days after giving birth, the mother stays at her parents' home, and then she will return to her husband and in-laws. But, for the first thirteen days, the mother and newborn child are left in a bedroom, to allow the mother to recover and bond with and learn to know her child – basically, she pretty much doesn't leave the bedroom for all those days. She is allowed the company of her relatives in the house, but the room is usually kept dark, and she is just in there alone with the baby. This was still being done in the 1990s (not followed so much these days), yet Money's parents had this in mind for me after I gave birth to Noah!

I didn't know anything about this, but several days before Noah was due, Pam came over.

'I'm so excited for you to come and stay with me once the baby is born,' she said.

What? I was about to give birth and she was expecting me to pack up everything and stay at hers with Noah?

Money and I got into a big argument once she had left.

'I compromised with you on living in our own house and you are not respecting me and compromising on this,' he said. He tried to explain that this ritual of thirteen days alone with the baby mattered, but because his mother didn't want me to be on my own to do it, and she wasn't sure my own mum would follow the ritual, she thought we should move in with her for me to do it there.

'It's nothing against your mum,' I explained, yet I didn't feel comfortable with any of it. But when Money's family has decided on something – and on top of that, when communication is very unclear – it is hard to be heard or understood. Money said he would try to tell his mother how I felt. I didn't think it was my job to do this. But he kept putting it off. And Pam kept pushing it and talking about how happy she was that I was coming to stay. In the end, none of this needed to have become so complicated if people had just talked to each other. Money *hadn't* told his mum what was going on because he didn't want to hurt her feelings. I was too scared to tell her, so she had no idea there was even this issue. When she realised it had become such a big deal that we actually weren't speaking to each other, a compromise was reached. She would stay with us for the thirteen days instead. All along I thought it was Pam causing the issues, but it was Money taking her side and pushing for this. He knew how much she wanted her 'grandparent time' after the birth and he didn't want to hurt her, but I wasn't being consulted.

Anything we have disagreed about, such as the matter of us moving into a joint family home, or Money's family thinking they would all turn up for Noah's birth, has practical reasons behind it within Indian society, where these arrangements make sense. That's why Money's family couldn't understand that this was not okay with me. Sometimes there are such differences because of how we have been raised. And any two people starting out will find this is the case, but when you add cultural differences into the mix, it can get so much trickier and be a lot more sensitive.

I urged Money from the start that if we argue, I need to do it in person, face to face, and get all my feelings out by talking. I need to be with someone who will communicate in a way where I leave the argument feeling better, rather than avoiding the issue so it comes up again in the next argument. Now we've come to a good solution where he will go upstairs and sit down and text me. He is scared to tell me things in person because he can get angry quickly and say things that are hurtful and that he regrets straightaway. But if he puts it in a text, he can delete things and take some time to say what is on his mind without overreacting. I can never just sit there and agree with him for the sake of it, and I have to discuss it. I am not even slightly hot-headed. Even if I am angry, I manage to stay calm and say what I have to say. But this was something we needed to work through. Now he can talk to me, sometimes, but if he is too upset or heated, he still prefers to go upstairs and text from there. So that is a good compromise we have reached about how we communicate. I can say, 'Text me and we will talk later.' And sometimes I will use his own way of communicating back to him. I might wait till he goes out and then I'll text him and ask, 'How can we fix this?'

My parents weren't like this. They had huge rows. It was probably being around them and witnessing how every argument ended up with someone saying they were leaving or the other person storming out of the house and nothing getting resolved that has made me so determined to find better ways of solving arguments. I can't see the point in shouting or letting things fester; I like to deal with them straightaway.

CHAPTER TWELVE

Introducing Noah

ABBEY

I was twenty-three when Noah was born. Lots of people have an opinion about whether it is better to be young parents or experience more life and then have children. It is a personal view; it isn't up to anyone else to say that one way is better than the other. For me, it was not about 'sacrificing my youth' as some have said – I never saw it like that. I only saw the benefits and I look forward to having grown-up kids while we are still relatively young. I want to be able to travel with Money and I feel happy knowing we're having our kids while in our twenties and have lots of energy to run around with them. It is what my mum did. When she was the age

I am now, she had three children. She loved being a young mother and said she could relate well to us because she was still quite close to those years as well. And Noah is so blessed that he has his grandparents around him who adore him and love spending time with him.

I have polycystic ovary syndrome (PCOS). I was diagnosed with it when I was quite young. My periods were always irregular, and I had bad acne, which is connected to this. Another alarming side effect is that it can make getting pregnant more difficult, so when we got married, I wanted to start trying as soon as possible. It would have always preyed on my mind to think I should have tried earlier if we had any trouble, so very early on we began 'Project Noah' – although we didn't yet know he was Noah. I was working at The Warehouse, studying full time and we were doing YouTube videos on the weekends. It didn't feel too hectic, but looking back, we were definitely pretty busy.

It was taking some time to get pregnant and everyone told me not to worry; the doctor reminded me I was young and it was common for it to take a while, even for women without PCOS. I was happy at The Warehouse, but my idea was, if I didn't get pregnant soon, I would look for a job in social work or become a parole officer. I wanted to continue to do a Master's degree, and these were good avenues to help with that. Then that very happy day came, finding out I was pregnant, and my plans changed. It made more sense to stay at The Warehouse. The management were awesome, taking me off any heavy-lifting jobs and giving me lots of cashier shifts. I was to go on maternity leave a month before the baby was due, in March 2020, and I'd get some rest and prepare for having a newborn.

Towards the end of 2019 we started to hear about this virus that was affecting parts of China and then it kept getting closer and closer to our borders. Then we went into lockdown in March. My heart sank because I knew I would be giving birth at Level 4 Covid restrictions. I would be cut off from my family when I needed them most, although it did mean Money was at home with me, which was really nice. He had been planning to take one week's paid leave, as this was all he had due, and then one week unpaid, but with Covid, he was off work. We went for walks every day and spent quality time together before the baby came.

I hadn't done any shopping for the baby because I thought I had maternity leave to do this. Pretty soon, I was online shopping for baby gear and essentials. I'm sure I was placing orders at Baby Factory nearly every day. Thankfully, they were regarded as an essential business and were doing deliveries. I obviously didn't have enough to worry about because I was even fretting that my orders would be delayed, but they came in time. In fact, everything happened that would have happened under normal circumstances, just in a different way, but the whole country was unsettled and getting used to what lockdown meant, let alone me being hormonal and anxious about giving birth in this strange environment.

When I had my check-ups, Money wasn't allowed to come with me. I had all the blood tests and scans on my own. I started imagining what it would be like if I found out something was wrong when he wasn't with me. Those appointments were horrible. Everyone was in masks and practising social distancing. I had to wait in the car with Money until I was called, then he waited there while I was in the consultation room. Our bubble was just the two of us. Mostly. Money saw his mum a couple of times. But those weeks were very hard. Pregnancy during lockdown was not ideal. My family couldn't come to see me, and when I went to see the midwife, Money couldn't come. I felt isolated and alone. It is not what you want, especially not for a first birth, and we had been so excited to share every moment of it together.

And then I went past my due date. I was so tired. And I was enormous. In fact, I was so huge that we decided to do a cast of my belly as a permanent record. We were going to video it for a laugh for our YouTube followers, and I was getting ready, doing my hair and makeup, when it dawned on me that for a few hours now I hadn't felt the baby kick. I tried the usual things to get him to move – going out, kerb walking, bouncing on a maternity ball, eating spicy foods – but nothing happened.

'Let's call the midwife,' said Money.

The midwife asked me to come straight to hospital, where she would meet me. Now our original plan of having our mums there, especially my mum as a trained midwife, went out the window. I had been relying on their assistance. We were also told that if Money had any flu symptoms or a temperature, not only would he not be allowed with me but also no other family member could replace him. I would be completely alone. This prospect really scared me. I made him wrap up and wear a facemask every time he left the house, because I couldn't face the prospect of going through labour by myself.

For a first childbirth, you are given so much information to remember but you don't know what to expect, so I didn't retain a lot of it. With me being worried about whether the baby was okay and everything around me so stressful, it is probably one of the reasons that I didn't go easily into labour. The midwife monitored me and said, 'You're eight days overdue and in a lot of discomfort, and it's not good that baby is moving less. We'll keep you in overnight and induce you tomorrow if nothing has changed.' This was the last thing I wanted but I didn't have much choice. The next morning, they moved me to a separate room for the induction, so at least Money was now allowed in. It eased my tense, stressed shoulders just seeing his face. He brought in lots of food, but I wasn't allowed to eat it in case I ended up having a Caesarean. They hooked me up to a hormone drip and asked if I wanted an epidural. Even though I'm really scared of needles, I had to do what was safest for the baby. The midwife explained that if I did need an emergency C-section it would be much easier if the epidural was already in. Also, giving birth after you've been induced is more painful because everything happens at once, so I agreed to it.

After a whole day, still nothing had happened. Noah didn't turn around and his heart rate was decreasing. The medical staff were concerned that the hormones they were giving me were putting added pressure on him. There were so many things going on. Then in a sudden rush and panic, I was being prepped for theatre. Baby was barely moving by now and I was to have a Caesarean. I signed the consent forms, and they told us Money could come in to theatre but, because of Level 4 Covid rules, he would have to leave the moment the baby appeared. He and I were a mess. I was signing my life away in case I went into cardiac arrest and was having an unscheduled C-section within Covid lockdown.

Money stayed and kept talking to keep me calm. He was amazing. He knew he couldn't do much to help, but he kept saying the sweetest things the whole way through and it did make everything better. And by now, Noah was so big that, even numbed by an anaesthetic, it still hurt so much! It felt like they were ripping out all my organs. It was the right decision to have a Caesarean. Noah weighed 10 pounds and I don't think I could have pushed him out if I had tried.

This is said often, I know, but the minute I saw our baby, nothing else mattered (although I was amazed that something that big had come out of me). In the end, Money was allowed to hold him for a couple of minutes, but then he had to leave. Suddenly, I was all alone again. And because they had taken my bag into my room, which had my phone in it, I couldn't contact anyone. I was in the recovery room for a very long time as they tried to get Noah to feed, but it wasn't going well. When I was finally wheeled into my room, the bag was over the other side of the room and no one thought to pass it to me and I was still numb and couldn't contact anyone to get help. There was just this little human being and me in an empty room. I couldn't move. I wanted to call my mum and show her Noah. I wanted to call Money. Noah was in a bassinette next to my bed and I couldn't even move to reach for him. I rang the bell for assistance, but nobody came.

It was terrifying and I never want to go through those feelings of helplessness again. What made it worse was that I hadn't slept for days because of the induction process, and so everything I was going through felt too big for me to handle. Like many new mums, I found feeding Noah difficult at first as he kept choking on the milk and making what I thought was an awful gurgling noise. I seemed to be always ringing the help button, and then that would make me feel bad for the nurses because they were overworked and understaffed and I was just one of many new mothers on their watch. And yet I didn't have my mum there and really needed their guidance.

Every time a nurse came, I asked them to let Noah stay in the bed with me as I couldn't move, but they wouldn't do that because it isn't safe. It was a very stressful three days with no sleep and not much help and I started to think I was going a bit crazy. Money was stuck at home, calling me constantly to see how Noah and I were doing and I didn't want to stay in hospital but didn't feel ready to go home. After three days, I was transferred to a facility that is like a halfway between hospital and home, and Money was finally able to come and visit us. In fact, their Covid rule was that once inside, Money couldn't come and go, so he stayed with us the whole time. Being together and for him to spend this time with Noah and me was the most special time ever.

Money was shaking and crying. 'Here's my son. Here's my son,' he kept saying.

There were still more issues and problems to deal with before we were in the clear. Noah was losing weight and was dehydrated, but at this facility, they were telling me I wasn't trying hard enough. They encouraged breastfeeding and frowned on formula for a baby, however, every time I fed him formula, he was more settled and he would stop crying. They'd argue with me again and tell me to try breastfeeding (which I was finding so hard and he did not want to latch). Someone there even had the audacity to suggest I had traumatised him by choosing to have a Caesarean.

I was constantly crying. Those comments from staff hurt and it shouldn't be allowed to happen to anyone. None of this is what I had planned and wished for. I wanted a natural birth and to be able to breastfeed, however, it hadn't worked out. I was coming to terms with this but I was already disappointed in myself without their judging.

In the end, Money called Mum. He was crying because I couldn't stop crying, and Noah was hungry so Noah was crying. Mum was livid. She rang the staff and demanded that they hand over formula immediately and added she was on her way over with more. She said I should discharge myself and go home and she would look after me night and day. We agreed. Mum was my guardian angel. She helped me learn to get Noah latched on and he put weight on really quickly. Before we knew it, he was breastfeeding happily, and still is, more than a year later. I was so lucky to have Mum to help me. It was such a stressful situation to go through and I can't imagine how hard it would be for those without that sort of support.

Because of the lockdown, people weren't allowed to come and visit us. I know this was difficult for the whole family who were keen to meet the new baby, but it did mean it gave me time to learn how to be a new mum and deal with all that stress without crowds of people watching our every move, giving their opinions on how things should be done. I did a couple of FaceTime catch-ups, and everyone else had to wait. During Noah's first month, we let only one or two people come at a time, but there was no kissing him. They could have a hold and then pass him back.

Everyone wanted to help. People were just incredible. We were so grateful for all the amazing help and generosity, and it meant I could focus on recovering. When there were days I had no energy to cook or shop, all we needed to do was ask and someone would do those things for us and leave deliveries in the letterbox or on the doorstep. In those first few days, Mum moved in to help get me sorted. My sister came too because she was in Mum's bubble. And Money's parents came because there was no way anyone was going to keep them from their first grandchild when we lived just minutes down the road and they weren't seeing anyone else anyway.

Holding my baby was mind-blowing. Noah was the most beautiful boy in the world and I cry every time I think about the birth. Definitely the hardest thing for me was the sleep deprivation. I am someone who needs a full eight to nine hours uninterrupted sleep every night and I was getting nowhere near that. And Noah was not one of those babies who just sleeps and feeds and sleeps. Well, he would feed, for eight hours at a time, then he might sleep for 20 minutes, wake up, play a bit and feed for three more hours. This is what they call 'cluster feeding', and it meant I was on call for many hours of the day and night.

It was the best time of my life, but it was the hardest time too. I wish I hadn't been so stressed, because that is most of what I remember now. I wish I had enjoyed it more. When you are pregnant, the build-up is all about the labour, but now I see what a small part that plays. I wish I had listened to my instincts and placed my trust in the hospital system to deliver our baby, instead of being so uptight and worried about everything. I was later diagnosed with post-partum depression, which is very common, and there can be so many reasons why this comes on – or there can be no tangible reason at all – but it is just there and has to be worked through. For me, with the whole birth experience and feeling unsupported in hospital and then coming home to find things weren't how I thought they would be, it all culminated in a very difficult period of my life. Becoming a mother is a hard job all on its own. I remember having vivid dreams of being in a car accident with Noah, and while awake, I had so much anxiety that something was going to happen to him. It got so I didn't want to take him out. I felt completely worthless and that I didn't matter at all and that no one heard or saw the pain I was in – especially when Money would see me crying and he didn't know what to do or say. I just wanted to disappear, but my responsibility to be there for Noah kept me showing up every day to do my best.

I think when Money went back to work and I was alone with Noah, I knew I had to get it together. I joined some mothers' support groups, and would take him to activities for babies (such as to the library every week, where we sang songs and did dances), and it was just so good to get out and socialise with other mums. That's when I started to feel confident in my new self and knew I could be a good mum. I took Noah out every day and we always kept busy and had the most amazing fun times together – and I wouldn't change a thing, honestly. He has completely changed my life for the better and I can't even put into words the amount that I love him – he is just my world! None of this was anything to do with Noah and, even at my lowest, all I felt was guilt for not being the best mum I could be – I never had any negative thoughts about him. I grew stronger and found my way and Money and I grew stronger and found our way. But, I accept fully that we had a tough time that we had to get through. It has made no difference to how Noah has grown, and he is a healthy, beautiful little boy. And I am trusting that I will learn from this experience for the future … which is now more real than ever, considering that as I write this I am pregnant with our second child.

CHAPTER THIRTEEN

Fatherhood

MONEY

I grew up in a culture where fathers didn't get involved in thc delivery of the baby or the raising of it. It was the women who did all the looking after, and with the tradition of extended family under the same roof, there was always someone around to help. But, as with many cultures, it was the mother who was expected to pick up the crying baby or change it. Never the father. In Indian households, the grandmothers and the father's sisters were available if they were still at home.

My mum was often working when I was a baby and it was other female relatives who looked after me, but by the time my brother came along, we were better off financially so my mother had more time to spend with him.

So, having a baby at home with just Abbey and me there was an eye opener. I loved being involved, but it was a steep learning curve, and I had to trust that I could do this role. As well, we felt that in choosing a love marriage and standing up for how we wanted to live our lives, we couldn't fall back into those traditional roles of what men do and what women do. I wanted to be a hands-on father. It also took me back to the days when Ash was born. I really love babies and I played a substantial role in his upbringing, like a father figure, so this gave me some confidence in raising my own child.

But nothing can prepare you for how life-changing it is when you first get to hold your baby. I will never forget it my whole life. Mum and Dad have told us how proud they are of the way we are raising Noah. But those early months were such hard work, as every new parent knows. We chose to put Noah onto a European baby routine early on, which meant that, as often as possible, seven o'clock in the evening was his bath and bedtime, no matter what else was happening in my family's calendar. This is not customary. The Punjabi community stay up late, including the babies, who get dragged along to whatever the parents are doing. When I was small, I would still be up, waiting for dinner at eight or nine at night.

Often, we didn't have dinner together as a family because Dad would finish work very late. My family found it strange to see us setting this routine. It'd be someone's birthday party, and they'd ask 'Why are you leaving? We haven't cut the cake.' But because everything is late, cutting that cake may not even happen before nine o'clock, and as much as we would have liked to help celebrate, we wanted to get Noah home. 'Sorry, we have to leave, it is our son's bedtime.'

They thought I had gone too far with this and they made comments that I wasn't involved enough in my family any more. But everything takes time to adjust. Now they can see how Noah is growing up and how he is benefitting from routine and structure, and perhaps they are beginning to think differently. If everyone gets to pick up a baby or the baby decides when they're ready for sleep and the parents aren't taking responsibility, it can create its own complications. Our way meant that, yes, we felt torn between what we wanted for Noah and what we wanted to do with our family, but we knew that Noah was getting regular play time, meal time, grandparent time, sleep time. And the good thing about structure and routine is that the parents get their time, too. They are not at the mercy of the baby every moment of the day and night.

Being a father is the best thing ever but it takes commitment and I have had to adjust my lifestyle. In my

Indian community, work and getting ahead in life are so important – they are first priority. But I have learnt that nothing is more important than the time you give your family. I also like that in the European tradition, the father is encouraged to be involved, from the labour pains through to the birth. That is not something I had ever seen growing up. In our culture, the woman usually goes back to her parents' house somewhere around her seventh month of pregnancy, which means the father isn't with her leading up to the birth. My mum said that with me, she thought she was in the seventh month but she was actually much later than this and when she arrived to stay with her parents, her doctor informed her she only had about two weeks until her delivery. She wrote a letter to my dad (this was the only means of communication) to come to her, so Dad and my *Dadi-ji* (Dad's mother) came one day before the delivery – but only one person was allowed in the delivery room for support and that ended up being my *Nani-ji* (Mum's mother).

There was one custom that I was supposed to follow when Noah arrived and I managed to stuff it up! When a child is born in our culture, a person in the family is chosen to give the baby raw honey. You have to put some on your little finger and gently rub some just on the baby's lip and inside his mouth. It is a symbolic way of saying 'I am giving my personality to this child', in the belief that they will grow up to be like the person who presents the honey. When I went to the hospital to see Noah for the first time, I had the honey from my mother, but I completely forgot all about it. Abbey and I had discussed it prior to the birth, and she chose that the honey should come from me so Noah would have my personality. I had it ready. We were in the labour room. She was trying to push. Then there was the emergency and into theatre. So who remembers anything at a time like that? Noah missed out on the honey. But he seems to be doing all right. Abbey thinks Noah has my personality anyway, so she thinks it has totally worked out in the end.

Like Abbey, I am now glad Noah's birth happened during Level 4 lockdown, otherwise we would have had so many visitors and no way of monitoring it. All the grandparents, all the aunties, would have been around and making a lot of noise while Abbey was trying to do what she needed to do, and it would have stressed her out so much. We were talking before the birth about how we could possibly have it be just me with her. I then had to tell my parents and they were so disappointed, especially my mum. This new baby meant so much to her, but Covid took the decision out of our hands.

Interracial couples definitely need to talk about how their baby will be brought up and how childcare will be managed *before* the baby arrives so that each parent feels respected and heard. We never talked about it in depth. We knew we wanted the grandparents involved, but even just saying that can mean something very different depending on which culture you are focusing on. 'Being involved' looked completely different to our two sets of parents. We didn't want Noah to be caught in the middle. We knew in our hearts what our families expected but we had never said it out loud to each other, so we had to do some pretty fast adjusting once we had the baby in the house.

We did not get off to a good start. On the day Noah was brought home, Mum wanted to do a special prayer over him, for cultural and religious reasons.

'I can't do a prayer right now,' said Abbey. 'I have just had an operation and I feel terrible.'

'Okay,' said Mum, 'we will delay the prayer.'

But even this took discussion, because with lockdown and the fears back then that we were all going to get Covid, just delaying the prayer for a week would still mean people in the house and potentially exposing a newborn to this virus. And this was on top of Abbey feeling irrational and tired and hormonal and bewildered all at the same time. My mum expected she would be on hand and involved with everything about the baby. Abbey was feeling like things were hard enough as it was, and felt that her wishes and what she needed weren't being considered, and that she was compromising for everyone else's happiness. The birth and the days after were very traumatic with feeding problems that meant Noah was not thriving as he should be. Abbey's mum stayed for the first three days and she was amazing. She was who Abbey was relying on.

After those initial couple of days, my mum stayed. Three weeks later, she was *still* there, and that is when the conflict started brewing. Abbey wanted her personal space, but there is no such thing as personal space in an Indian household. We're used to extended family staying – for years, if necessary. These are the sort of interracial issues you don't think about until you are in the middle of trying to fix them. When my dad and brother were visiting our home, Abbey didn't feel comfortable breastfeeding with them in the room. They'd bring a meal for us all to eat, but Abbey would go into the bedroom to feed Noah. She could hear everyone else eating and enjoying themselves, and she knew her meal would be cold by the time she got to it. I'd sit with them but didn't eat, waiting to have a cold meal with Abbey.

There were lots of mixed messages. I understand how Abbey felt. But I also knew an Indian person wouldn't be able to understand why we didn't want my mum in the house every day. I guess one of the reasons we didn't talk about everything beforehand was that we didn't know what it would be like. We didn't know what we needed to talk about. We will know with the next baby. And it made it worse that everyone was trying to help and wanting to do what was best for Abbey and Noah, but they just had different ideas about what 'best' meant. Everyone was overthinking everything, and no one was saying clearly what they needed.

Mum kept offering to do things for Abbey. 'Would you like me to massage your hair or your legs? I know every part of you will be hurting after having a baby.' It was all done with love, but the cultural differences were now just massive.

'Mum is trying to help you,' I explained. 'She is doing it for you.'

And even though Abbey knew it was coming from a place of kindness and that Mum was just anxious to help, Abbey was in pain and didn't want to be touched by anyone – including me. There was so much mental anguish and Abbey felt like her space was being taken over.

I needed to think about me, too. I was in the middle, trying to keep everyone in my life happy. I was learning to be a father and I would never get this special time back. I felt bad cutting Mum out because I had already disobeyed my parents by marrying out of my culture, so I was never able to tell my mum straight up what I wanted, or what Abbey wanted. I just let it be – it's what I do really well: avoid the conflict and keep quiet. I am the kind of person who prefers to let time fix fights. Even though I have worked on my communication skills, when Abbey and I argue she is still the one who does most of the talking. But now, I had to put my foot down where the baby was concerned and that was hard. I felt sick with dread over what I had to say to my mum, so I kept putting it off and not being clear to anyone. This frustrated Abbey, of course, who kept waiting for me to stand by her and do as she was pleading, which was for them to go home and give her some space.

Eventually I explained to Mum that if she could just go home for the night to give us some time on our own with the baby, we think this would be a good thing for everyone. She started crying. I started crying. She did not take it well. She said she didn't want to come back the next night. I felt like this wouldn't be happening if I had agreed to an arranged marriage. Whenever Mum is hurt, it hurts me. It was back to having to choose sides. I felt very desperate. My mental health was on a knife-edge and perhaps a lot was coming to the surface that hadn't been sorted through since those first huge arguments, but I was very low.

Surprisingly, it was my dad who was there for me. Since recovering from the drama about our relationship and accepting Abbey, he has been very understanding. I was sitting in the garage crying when he came in.

'Money, what are you crying about?' he asked. 'You haven't done anything wrong.'

'I feel I've let you guys down. I can't cope with everything.'

'No, you haven't. And Abbey is the sweetest girl. She loves you, and she will be a good mother. We just don't understand these cultural differences.'

Then Mum joined us and Dad told her, 'He's not kicking you out of the house. He just wants some space. Give them some space.'

'My grandson will not know me,' cried Mum. She wasn't trying to take over, she wanted to do her duty and felt like she was being prevented from doing so. There is a strong cultural belief in her that she was clinging to. Children can be in everyone's life when they are older, but for the first couple of years, the important adults in that child's life need this bonding time.

Eventually, a compromise of sorts was reached: Mum was there every day and spent a lot of time with Noah, and after dinner she would go home. But still none of that time was easy. Those first few weeks were the hardest of our relationship. They were even harder to deal with because up until then we'd really not had any problems. We'd managed to sort everything: our relationship, the marriage announcement, the wedding, even the social media – it all took work but we always reached an agreement. We were a good team. But once Noah was born and we brought him home, we never dreamt it would be this hard. We already had so many emotions to deal with as parents of a newborn baby without all these other compromises to make on top of that.

It took a long time but we worked hard on our relationship and now we look back and feel proud that we managed to get through it and come out the other side stronger and closer than ever. When Noah was about two months old, Abbey was diagnosed with post-partum depression, which was a major hurdle to deal with. She was going through so much. You wouldn't think to look at my beautiful happy boy today that there has been any difficulty at all in his short life so far. That shows how amazing children are, and how amazing my beautiful, happy wife is, because she battled on, she kept all of that away from Noah, and she is so strong. She pulled herself through it. And I guess I helped where I could – especially when I learnt to speak up.

CHAPTER FOURTEEN

A Home of Our Own

ABBEY

It is our Sikh belief that when you acquire a big asset, the first thing you must do is thank God. When we bought our house, we had a *path* (pronounced 'part'), which is a Sikh blessing ceremony. There are many special occasions where a *path* might be used. There was one for our wedding, for instance. You can get one when you receive your citizenship. A child's birthday can be another reason. A *part* ceremony lasts from one to three days, takes a lot of planning and is a very big deal.

We went to the temple and asked the *Granthi* to come to our house. Everyone from the *Gurdwara* was invited and all were welcome, which is the Sikh way. Money's dad was so proud that his son had been able to purchase a house; he got a bit carried away and was inviting anyone he could: 'Here is my son's address. They are having a *path*. Please come by.'

Money had to say, 'Dad, please don't keep giving our address to everyone.'

We waterblasted the driveway and cleaned the house from top to bottom, so it would be fit to take the *Guru Granth Sahib* (holy book). We cleared the house of alcohol, and smoking and eating meat were also prohibited because the holy book was under our roof. In other words, your home temporarily becomes a *Gurdwara*. When the *path* took place in our living room, chapters of the *Guru Granth Sahib* were read aloud, around the clock, by the *Granthi*. There was reading and singing, and *kirtan* (the music of God), drumming and praying.

On that day, 120 people walked through our new home. The living room, the hall, the kitchen, the whole of upstairs – everywhere was packed with people. You couldn't move for people. It was our responsibility to provide a *seva*, which means service or hosting, so that meant breakfast and lunch for all the visitors. Money's family (aunties, uncles, cousins, parents) went to the *Gurdwara* the night before and they prepped all the food for the next day. They are just incredible, the way everyone pitches in and helps. For breakfast we served *pakora* (vegetable fritters), *aloo* toast (fried potato bread), Indian sweets (*barfi, jalebi, ladoo*), and for lunch there was *chole bhature* (chickpea curry), *mutter paneer* (pea and Indian cheese curry), *daal* (lentil curry) and salads and *roti*. It was a long day. People just came and went as they pleased the whole time and, as part of the *path*, they brought gifts. At its completion, the house is purified and made safe and refreshed for the new homeowners.

With some *path*, there is the option of holding it at the *Gurdwara*, but with a house-warming, it needs to be on your premises. The purpose of it is to welcome *Baba Ji* (God) into your home. Basically, we are saying we owe everything to him and want to thank him for all the blessings he has given us including this new home. We are inviting him into the home, saying, 'This home is also your home and please help us look after it and look after those inside.' Following the Sikh religious customs so closely like we did that day made Money's parents so proud and happy. In the past, it was these sort of occasions they really worried about: if it wasn't an arranged marriage, would we know or agree to follow the rituals? It is lovely they can see that, yes, it really matters to us as well. My mum and my sister also came that day. I loved seeing our two families together, supporting us.

Once the *path* was finished, we had to clean the house all over again because there were stains everywhere from having so any people trampling through and eating and drinking. Noah was still so little when this took place, and I had to keep going up and down to his bedroom, trying to get him to sleep while music was playing loudly and people kept going into his room on the house tour and to see him.

I think we are truly blessed. It is a beautiful, warm, sunny home, with good outside space for us to hang out in. We are so fortunate. And it makes our families really happy – especially how we managed to find somewhere near them. When Noah was really tiny, I'd walk from where we were living in the rental over to Money's parents' house every day and spend hours there so they could have time together. It was important to me that Money's family see how much we wanted them in our lives. Now that this home is also close by, we are always at each other's places and Noah gets so excited when any members of the family come to visit. It is very special to have this home and be able to share it.

MONEY

Finding a house and negotiating the sale is a very stressful time and, for us, it was more difficult because we only wanted to look at houses close to our parents. The North Shore area was becoming expensive, as were all house prices in Auckland, no matter the suburb. I left it to God and knew that whatever he wanted for us would be good.

Then when we found a house we both liked that met all our requirements and we put in an offer, we were gutted when we didn't get it.

'God has other plans for you,' Mum reminded us.

He did, because another house came up that we liked, and after a lot of back and forth between real estate agent and vendor and us, our offer was accepted. We had to wait another seven days to finalise the contract and every one of those days we drove past it. They were still holding open-house inspectionses and we prayed none of the people looking would want it. Fortunately, they didn't, and the house was ours.

Home ownership matters in our culture. Our family home in Bowani is my great-grandfather's house, which passed to my grandfather, who then passed it on to his sons. My dad and his brothers had this house completely renovated, but they did so from Auckland, so they'd call back and forth with the builders and, occasionally, they went over to check on the progress. Money's grandmother has been able to go back to India and see it, which is so good as it was a dream of hers to get this done. The house is beautiful now. In the village, there is a poor family who lived nearby and my dad and uncle gave the keys of the house to them so they could live there rent-free and look after it for us now that our family has moved to New Zealand.

Home ownership is just as important here, too. As soon as my uncle and Dad had earned enough money, the first thing they did was buy a house. On the day they took ownership, they began the process of subdividing the property so that as family came out, they also could live there.

Purchasing a house was always part of our own plan for setting ourselves up to have a family and to feel secure but, of course, it had to have some family drama along the way. After we got married in 2018, I knew I wanted full-time work, which meant leaving The Warehouse, as my role there was part-time. My second-hand clothing business wasn't a long-term option, so I sold my stock and database on the TradeMe website.

In February 2019, I began working at Noel Leeming as a tech solutions specialist. This meant going into customers' homes and showing them how to use the technology and equipment they had bought from us. There was also some sales work. If a customer had a budget of $5000 and wanted a new computer and sound system, we would work out what would suit their lifestyle, how it would fit their budget, and then we'd install it and show them how it worked.

It was a happy place to work. People were always pleased to see us: we had their new product to install. Also, they tended to be elderly people and I liked helping them, and they had stories to share and treated me so well, offering me a cup of tea sometimes. This suited my culture, where we're brought up to enjoy and respect the company of older people. Our elders don't go into retirement homes, but remain with their children and grandchildren. I was always told that no matter what happened, say between my uncle and Dad if they were arguing, I was not to get involved or say anything. Children do not interfere in their parents' fights, so my Noel Leeming customers never had to worry about me not respecting them, even if I knew more about some things than they might.

While my hours were 8 am to 6 pm, an advantage to the job was that, sometimes, there was spare time during the day when I wasn't out on a job when I could work on our social media channel, which meant I could be with Noah and Abbey at night rather than still have lots of editing to do. But the regular work was also enough to get us a mortgage – just. By this stage, we were earning money from YouTube, but no one in our family understood this, and neither did the banks. YouTube income is confusing for a bank; it is still reasonably unknown as a way of earning money in New Zealand. There are no invoices created – the money just gets put in your account. It is possible to look up and analyse the statistics, but the bank kept coming up with reasons not to factor this in as part of our mortgage application.

'That's not real income,' was their explanation.

'What do you mean? You can see the actual amount in our account.'

'You need to show you can earn this much for six months.' Then, 'You need to show you can earn this much over one year.' They would ask hypothetical questions such as, 'What if your followers left you and you weren't able to make that money any more?' The reason I stayed with Noel Leeming as long as I did was that the income satisfied the bank's expectations. Then social media began taking up so much of my time and, sometimes, I was getting offers for YouTube sponsorships that paid more than I was getting at Noel Leeming – it was time to re-evaluate.

The assumption that Indian people work really hard is absolutely true. No one ever sits around doing nothing. There is always some hustle going on in order to provide for the family. In our culture, we don't have a problem admitting that money is important and that we care about it. We have to. None of us is living only for today or only for ourselves. I think when you come from a society with a lot of poverty, money provides the necessities, but more, it can buy a lifestyle and it enables you to help others. In our family, we are always saving and preparing – first, for our own future and, second, our children's future. My dad would never think about retiring. He made money for himself and my mother, then he wanted to make money to set up me and Ash. Now he is talking about needing to make money for Noah and future grandchildren. He doesn't have any personal indulgences; he wants the best for his family. Once my parents' business in the clothing industry was sound, they still didn't spend their money. They bought a house, but not a new house in an expensive area. Dad had the same car for fifteen years before he passed it on to me. As a child, I saw or understood only a small part of this picture. I watched my uncle reach a certain financial position when he could then buy new stuff, but Dad kept getting us second-hand gear. Why? I gave him a hard time, but Dad was content with the way he was managing things. Now, one of the reasons I want to earn money is so I can buy things for Dad, but it's not easy and he is stubborn. He had to change his car recently and I wanted to buy him one but he wouldn't let me.

Mum has always worked hard, too. She sewed for a tailoring business in India and then here in New Zealand. She made clothes for the family, and she sews curtains for people. She's so resourceful. My aunties and female cousins wanted their eyebrows done for special occasions, and so now my mum does this after she taught herself how to do threading. Then people asked her if she would do facials for them, so she bought some equipment and learnt the techniques. She has turned one of the rooms in their home into a beauty salon for family and friends – and on the wall, in pride of place, is the framed picture of the Golden Temple that Abbey gave her the first time they met. Mum never buys herself anything, either; she is saving it all for the kids.

I've listened and watched people's assumptions about work and income, especially along cultural divides within New Zealand. We have our reasons for working so hard at what looks like menial work. A dairy owner will know it also means a job for their kids after school, and the grandfather has a turn behind the counter and feels he is contributing. Indian people don't retire. Why would we if we can keep making money for our families? We know the comments that are made, but we keep our own counsel. Did you ever wonder why you never saw Apu's house on *The Simpsons*? I liked Apu, even though he became a controversial character. I thought he was funny. And he was like every Indian person I know. Everyone in the Springfield community knew him and he always worked hard and tried not to cause any drama, but he gave very little away about himself. The crazy thing is that on *The Simpsons*, there was just as controversial a Scottish character, Groundskeeper Willie, with his kilt and his flaming red hair. Funny how both Abbey and my cultures are represented in that TV show.

The example set by Mum and Dad and my extended family has had a huge influence on me, but me wanting to leave Noel

Leeming immediately caused problems and everyone became involved. Not having a 'regular' job went against what my parents believed. Abbey wanted me to leave work and she could clearly see the logic behind the decision. 'You are editing at night, you are not getting enough sleep, and you have no time to do what you want, nor be with me and Noah.'

But with my parents, it was drama. They didn't get it, despite how many times I tried to explain it. I told Mum first. 'Don't quit. You have a good job,' she said, knowing she was speaking for them both. But she ended up understanding it from our perspective. She does trust that I know what I am doing and will make the right choices, even if at first she refuses to accept it. Abbey says it is because Mum and I are basically the same person.

'Why not just switch to part-time to be safe?' Dad kept saying. He thought YouTube was a nice hobby. 'You have taken on a home loan and you have a baby now. These are responsibilities you must ensure you can cover and be able to pay for.'

'God has given us this opportunity,' I said. 'We don't know how long the social media thing will last, but it will last longer if I do it properly. If it comes to nothing, I will always be able to find another job.'

One day I came home from work and told Abbey I had quit. She had been telling me to leave Noel Leeming for so long that when I finally did, she was a bit shocked. But she was proud of me too. And my parents have finally learnt about YouTube and how we earn our money. And they now see that I'm as responsible for my family's future as they were for us.

'No matter what you earn, never tell anyone,' said Mum, once they understood it more. 'I don't want this going to your head. Don't show off. Never brag. Stay humble. Remember why you are doing this and that God gave it to you. When God gives, he gives with his arms wide open.'

Abbey and I are sensible with money and, God willing, we will always stay humble. Before I left Noel Leeming, we had saved up enough to ensure that we could pay our mortgage from our savings for the next two years. Just in case anything went wrong with this new arrangement, we had to have this back-up plan. We would have found it too stressful without the security and peace of mind. And I have always had two bank accounts, in separate banks: one for spending and one for saving. We never look at or touch the savings account but it is reassuring to know it is there: those rainy-day funds people talk about. Over time, we switched banks to one that understood an online presence better.

So, I left my regular job, after much negotiating with my parents until they saw and trusted that we'd be okay –

and then, recently, when my brother who has also been working at Noel Leeming found it didn't suit him anymore, Dad shrugged and suggested he should just leave and find somewhere else! That's how it's been – I break the barrier and Ash walks on through the gap. You've got to laugh.

CHAPTER FIFTEEN

Worlds Apart, Families Together

ABBEY

People have this idea that I *have* to be involved in Money's culture or that my Scottish heritage doesn't matter to me. None of this is true, although I'm definitely enjoying all the sides to Money's Indian culture and am keen to learn more.

I already know how to do Scottish dancing, so I'm finding it more fun teaching myself Punjabi dances at the moment, specifically *bhangra* and a little bit of *gidda*. I've been mainly learning them at home where I watch people online or I learn with Money's family. The music and the dance moves make me feel so alive and full of energy – I smile so much every time I dance them because the happiness it gives you is unreal. I felt like I just clicked with it the minute I started learning and it's become one of my favourite things to do. It would be a laugh to take Money to a highland dancing workshop, but I've never been able to find one. But actually, when I was growing up I learnt Irish dancing because my grandmother is Irish. She was really good at it, and Mum also won lots of dance medals when she was young. I loved it, too. My hair would be in these tight curls and the outfits were amazing – long-sleeved dresses and an underskirt that makes them flare out. One of my plans some day is to try and incorporate Irish dancing with *bhangra*. I think it would be so fun to see if it works. We could make a video of it.

The most Scottish thing Money could learn to cook is haggis, but he doesn't need to because I am not a fan. I've only eaten it once, at a shared lunch at school. If you don't know what it is, it's minced heart, liver and lungs from an animal, usually a sheep, and in the olden days, they'd use the cleaned stomach lining as the cooking bag – I *know*! These days, the bag is usually synthetic. The minced meat has oatmeal, onions, suet and heaps of seasonings and spices mixed in and then it is cooked until it is like crumbly sausage. To be more Scottish, you would serve it with neeps (mashed turnip), tatties (mashed potato) and wash it down with a wee dram of whisky. *Ah dinnae ken,* why anyone would want to eat that, but there you go. Money used to say he was keen to try making it, but he might not if he saw what goes into it. It would make another good YouTube video though.

And I don't think he should try learning the bagpipes, for our sake or our neighbours', but he did look really handsome in the Scottish tartan waistcoat at our wedding, so maybe we should get him into a kilt – although Money doesn't like his calves. Another plan is to get matching kilts made for Money and Noah. They would look adorable in them. It would take some work to source this; I only know of one kilt-making store in Auckland and it is ages away and not many kilts come in kids' sizes. Just like the beautiful *lengha*, there's a lot of tradition about the fabric – each family or clan or region in Scotland has their own tartan plaid. To make a kilt properly takes hours and hours – they're very complicated.

The Indian community here in Auckland is so large they are able to come together to celebrate all the Indian festivals on the calendar. I could also drive to Papatoetoe this minute and find more than sixty Indian stores and buy matching outfits for the whole family, and within a small radius of where we live are three Indian food stores. In Auckland, Money could choose to live a life similar to one back home in India if he wanted. I guess I do wish there were more

Scottish things for us to do, but it just isn't the same. I loved it when we went to Wellington to see the military tattoo with the replica Edinburgh Castle and massed pipes. Even though it was nothing compared to what the tattoo is like in Edinburgh, it was the next best thing. I hope we can take Noah to Scotland some time, because I want him to grow up knowing that side of his heritage. I've shown him the Edinburgh tattoo on YouTube and played the music for him, but for the full impact of it, you need to be there in person.

Our YouTube followers often say they want to see more of my Scottish culture, but when we give it a go and put it online, we don't get as many views. It seems more popular when we try to mix the cultures up, which is what we love, too. I now have a strong connection to three countries, which can be confusing when it comes to which one I call 'home' but, really, New Zealand is my home. It made me who I am and my happiest memories are here. Most of all, I found my husband here. Scotland is like the roots of my tree, and New Zealand is the tree itself. India holds a special place in my heart, even though I haven't physically been there yet. We really want to visit India and, even though it will be a culture shock for me in many ways, I think it will somehow feel familiar as well. It would be great to see Money's relatives who made the trip out to attend our wedding, and meet more of his family. Money says that when I am there, people will try to haggle with me in shops and they'll be shocked when I haggle back in Punjabi.

It is my family in my home country that is the biggest pull for me back to Scotland, rather than the things that make me Scottish. One of the hardest times was when my grandfather died, in 2018. He had been quite sick and had dementia, and when I visited, the year before, I would sit with him, but it wasn't easy and I didn't really know what to say or do. He didn't know who I was any more. I tried to explain that I was his granddaughter, and I didn't think the message wasn't getting through, but then we left for New Zealand and Granny told me that he woke up one morning and asked if Abbey was coming to see him. Granny was astonished. It broke my heart to be so far away. It still hurts that I didn't get to see him and hug him one more time.

His health deteriorated really quickly, and on the day he passed away, Granny called us via Facebook. 'I know today is the day,' she said, sadly. 'Take the time to tell him what you have to say, he doesn't have long.' And we watched him slip away while we were on the call. It was really peaceful. He took a deep breath and, although he hadn't been opening his eyes for a long time, just at the end he did open them, he looked at my granny and tried to touch her face. Then he took his last breath. We stayed on the call with Granny until a friend arrived with communion for her because she wasn't able to go to church. My dad was nearby and came, so she wasn't entirely alone but she didn't have her children or us there.

Mum reacted instantly. 'I'm going there now,' she said. 'Your granny is on her own in that house.' And she booked a flight. She wanted to get there as soon as possible and it is a long trip – from Auckland to Dubai to London to Glasgow, and then a drive from there to Bellshill. Mum really wanted to support her mother and help with the funeral arrangements. We hoped Granny might move here once Grandpa had died, but he is buried there and Granny won't leave him, even now.

Mum did manage to bring her back for about a month after the funeral, which was incredible. Because Mum works full time and had used up a lot of leave with this trip to Scotland, Granny spent much of her time with Money and me at our flat, and we just had the best time together. We played Yahtzee and did lots of baking and cooking. Money and I had not been married long at the time and it felt like my grandmother wanted to pass on to me her ideas of what makes a good wife. I know that sounds very old-fashioned, but I guess there are similarities to what a traditional marriage within the Punjabi culture expects. My grandparents had been together since they were 16 and she took amazing care of Grandpa – he was her whole world, as she was his. Perhaps teaching me was her way of reliving some of those times, because she talked about thoughtful gestures she used to make and she said she was giving tips to make a happy home. Things like making sure dinner is ready and warm when Money gets home, folding the washing nicely, making his lunch. She even took me out to buy a lunchbox for Money because he had started his new job at Noel Leeming then.

It was so sweet, and even if Money and I are working out our own ways of helping around the house and being a partnership, I will never forget her kindness and advice to me and those precious days together. Granny is still living on her own in Bellshill. I miss her every single day. I wish she could live with me and Money in our home and I could look after her as she has looked after others all her life.

Covid has complicated things for many families and especially those with elderly relatives. Money also has family members in India who are not in the best of health and he would love to see them again. Granny is too scared to leave the house because of the pandemic. She has been dreadfully isolated, but her neighbours have been so kind, checking on her through the window and doing as much as they can for her. Thankfully, even at the age of eighty-two, she knows how to use her iPad and we FaceTime a lot. It's not the same as having her here, but it's better than nothing. She adores

Noah and is always thrilled to be able to see him and chat to him online.

MONEY

Sharing our culture and learning about each other's has been a major part of our lives and a regular theme on social media because people enjoy it. There is so much humour when we get things wrong, and a lot of pride from us – and from our viewers – when we get things right. Something that does really well on TikTok is when I test Abbey's Punjabi. When she first counted from one to ten, on a video clip, people were amazed. 'What – she is learning Punjabi?' It is pretty amazing, because she is so quick at picking it up and it is a very difficult language to learn if you haven't grown up around it. And there are tricky grammatical issues such as that a verb is different depending on whether a male or a female is performing the action. If Abbey gets that wrong when she is talking in Punjabi because she is copying a phrase from me and using the words I've used, we get a flood of comments saying, 'Hang on, you are not a male, you can't use that word.' So we can tell that people are interested and taking note.

Abbey has learnt mainly from listening to me and my parents, and she can understand nearly everything we say when we are speaking Punjabi. Now she wants to keep working on her speaking skills, but when we tried to find classes, the only option was at the *Gurdwara*, where they have lessons for young children, which didn't suit. She is very modest about her skills, but she obviously has an aptitude for languages. Now that we are teaching Noah, she is speaking more of the language with him, and she says that has helped to motivate her to keep learning. And she is learning about the Sikh religion and Punjabi culture. It is a beautiful sign of respect. One thing we love is when they show Indian movies at the Auckland picture theatre. It is such a great vibe. As soon as there's a dancing scene, everyone in the theatre goes wild and we all get up and dance along. It's crazy, like we're part of the movie, not just watching the actors on screen.

I am proud that we have inspired others to think more about the languages they speak. Often interracial couples tell us they've been together a long time and haven't made much effort to learn about their partner's culture, and we've made them want to do this. We get many, many messages from people asking us how we do it, how Abbey is learning Punjabi, and so on, so we can see that this aspect of our lives is reaching far and wide. It will be interesting to see how Noah handles all this as he grows up. He might be like my brother – when Ash speaks English he has a perfect New Zealand accent; when he speaks Punjabi, it is with a full Indian accent.

It has been easier for me because I was used to a European lifestyle growing up in New Zealand, whereas Abbey didn't know anything about Indian culture until she met me, so hers was a crash course, in comparison. I admire Abbey so much for the way she has adapted to a culture that is so different from her own. I've enjoyed the aspects of Scottish culture I've been shown, and I really loved being able to get to Bellshill and meet some of Abbey's family, to see where she grew up and to meet her grandmother and her father. I've even tried haggis, although only the kind that comes in a can. There aren't as many unique Scottish foods as there are Indian ones. I have tried making shortbread for Abbey a few times but I keep burning it.

Abbey's mum is very proud of her heritage. She booked us all tickets to Wellington one time to go and see the Royal Edinburgh Military Tattoo. It was incredible – hundreds of dancers and marching and drumming and more bagpipes than you can ever imagine. Not many people know this, but bagpipes are a traditional part of folk bands in India, and so it is a sound I am used to. More unusual for me was staying in a cottage that Abbey's mum had hired. When Indian families travel away from their home, we don't stay in hotels. We either do day trips or go to places where we have family and stay with them. We even take our own food and eat like we would at home. Staying in a hotel and dining out and trying different foods doesn't happen and I liked giving all this a go. I got a lot out of having a European-style holiday, and being with the family, because Abbey's brother and sister were on that trip as well.

Language and traditions are two aspects our cultural differences; Sikhism is another. There are five outward signs that someone is a Sikh, all beginning with k: *kesh*, uncut hair; *kara*, a bracelet; *kangha*, a comb; *kachera*, underpants made of cotton; and *kirpan*, a dagger or a small ornamental item. I want to point out that I am not *sardar* or *amritdhari*. A *sardar* is a Sikh who wears a *pagri* (turban) and doesn't cut their hair (but they could cut their beard if they like). An *amritdhari* is someone fully devoted to the religion who follows those traditions, doesn't cut their beard or any hair on their body, is also wholly vegetarian and adheres to the Five Ks of Sikhism; they are the kind of person that would usually be a *Granthi* or play *kirtan* (music) at the *Gurdwara*. It is important to mention that someone could adopt the full traditions and convert to these roles later in life even if they had previously cut their hair or eaten meat, for example.

People quiz me online about my religion. 'Why did you cut your hair?' 'Why did you shave your beard?' 'Why don't you stand up for our culture more? Our gurus fought for our rights to wear the turban, and they should be respected.' I can only answer for myself. I know that moving to a very different culture and environment early on, and being bullied for wearing the *patka* when I was younger, has played its part. I wanted to fit in. I didn't see the significance of all of it when I was a child and I didn't have the maturity to listen to my elders. I was just going my way and learning to be on 'both sides of the fence', as that was the only way I knew how to cope.

The word 'Singh' is very significant, and you know if you see someone wearing a turban, his surname will be Singh, but we got a lot of heat online about Abbey not changing her last name to Kaur when we got married. Abbey chose to follow her family's European tradition, which is that the bride usually takes the groom's surname, so Abbey chose to be 'Abbey Singh'. The other common way nowadays is for the bride to keep her own name, or link it with the groom's name, so she could have still been Abbey Brown, or Abbey Brown-Singh. The important thing is, it was Abbey's decision to make and changing her surname to Singh is what she chose.

Primarily, being Sikh is about believing in one God. We are a welcoming religion and anyone can come into the *Gurdwara*; our doors are always open. In every temple there is a copy of the *Guru Granth Sahib*, used in all ceremonies, and it is full of wisdom and knowledge. We have one God, but 10 gurus. These are not deities – they are historical holy men whose teachings are the foundation of our beliefs. I love my Sikh faith, but it is not as strong for me as it is for my parents' generation. When my uncle was thinking about coming to New Zealand, he went to the temple and asked for guidance about what he should do. He was told that all his family would eventually settle in New Zealand.

Mum's faith is strong. When I was less than a year old, Mum remembers that I had these red blisters all over my leg that just appeared out of nowhere and no one could explain them. A doctor told Mum they would have to be burnt off but warned her the procedure could cause paralysis or cost me my life. 'There is nothing else you can do,' he said.

'Well, I won't agree to that,' said Mum. 'I'm going to the *Gurdwara* to seek help.'

At the temple, she was given a prayer to repeat every day and told to walk up and down the temple stairs and devote herself to God. After a month of this, the blisters disappeared. Since then, Mum has been very devout. She believes that whenever you need something, if you pray with a clean heart, then good things will happen. I believe that, too.

CHAPTER SIXTEEN

Raising Noah

ABBEY

We named Noah according to a Sikh practice called *hukumnama*, which means 'royal decree'. When a decision needs to be made or a question answered, the *Guru Granth Sahib* is often used for spiritual guidance and wisdom. We chose the Golden Temple as our *Gurdwara* to give us the first letter, and from there we could name our child. At the end of the *ardas* (the request), the holy book is opened at random, and the first *shabad* (hymn or section of text) that appears on the left-hand page is the answer. We had a few names picked out that we liked, but our favourite name was Noah, so we couldn't believe it when the letter N was the first letter on the page we opened. After following *hukumnama*, it is perfectly okay to choose a Western name. Noah also has the middle names of his grandfathers who have passed away, William and Inder, with Singh as his surname. There were so many comments online about our choice of name for him, some liking it, some not, some questioning why we gave him that name – but we love it and it suits him so well. It's amazing how quickly we couldn't imagine him being called anything else.

We hadn't thought all that much about religion before Noah was born. We don't go to *Gurdwara* every week, but when we do, we take him with us so he will have lots of exposure to Sikhism. We want him to explore all religions but, more, we want him to have a good heart and be kind. I think people focusing on teaching kids about one specific religion can be limiting, rather than teaching them how to be good people. If he is a good person, the world will look after him.

As Noah grows up, my family will show him more of his Scottish side and Money's will show him more of his Indian side, and together we will bring him up as a New Zealander – which definitely means giving him opportunities to know Māori culture as well. We speak to him every day in Punjabi and English, and we've been reading him children's books written in te reo and teaching him Māori words and greetings, especially as these are the years when he will pick up languages the quickest. Money says he remembers being in the kapa haka group at his primary school, performing on stage and wearing the piupiu, and that they were some of the best times of his life. We give Noah both European and Indian foods to eat, every day, and we might put something like the military tattoo on YouTube for him to clap and dance in front of. One day, he will begin to notice that the people in his life do different things and start to ask why.

A big example of doing things differently was about his hair. Noah had his first haircut when he was nine months old. If we followed only Money's culture, this may not have happened for many years or perhaps his hair may have never been cut. From my perspective, it wasn't my place to have an opinion on a belief this personal to Money and his family. Money felt like he didn't want to enforce something on Noah that he wasn't committed to himself, like his father before him. As Noah's hair grew, it was getting in his ears and annoying him, so one day we just decided to cut it. If he wants to grow his hair later, we will encourage it but for now we think this is easier. We did a vlog about the haircut at the time and tried to explain our reasons, while being careful not to say what we thought others should do. We never want to present ourselves as role models for anyone. We are just us. We expected a lot of backlash about Noah's haircut but people were very respectful and lovely about it.

When we planned to get married, our mothers' attitudes were very different. Money's parents wanted us to make a wedding date straightaway; my mum wanted me to finish my studies and set ourselves up for our future and not rush into it. Very early on, Money's mum began talking about how she was looking forward to becoming a grandmother; this didn't even enter my mum's head. She wanted me to live some more life first. Then we got married and had Noah, and both of them were immediately on the same page – smitten grandmothers.

It then seemed that in no time at all Noah was turning one. We planned a huge celebration – actually we ended up having three celebrations – which is becoming the way of things around here. Respecting our cultures often involves doubling or even trebling up, but we like to make sure no one is left out. I also saw this as my own personal celebration – my tribute for beating post-natal depression. Getting through this first year was a real milestone, and Noah's birthday became a lovely time to reflect on that. It had been a tough time, we were starting to know what it meant to be parents, and we were surrounded by love from family and friends. It was time to party!

The first one was a typical European-style kid's birthday party, with a bouncy castle and too much food and Noah's little friends there, along with their parents, and just heaps of chaos and fun. Noah had an amazing day. He didn't come near Money or me the whole time because there were so many others he wanted to be with. And then he fell into an exhausted sleep.

Next, we had a celebration for the immediate family: both sets of grandparents, and Ash and my sister. This was held on Noah's actual birthday, 20 April, at an indoor playground. Again, he was overstimulated by noise and too many things to do and eat, and we let him go wild.

Two days after that, there was a full Indian celebration, which is a bit like a wedding, and is great fun, but there is not a lot in it for a one-year-old. It's at nighttime, with alcohol and food, drunk uncles and dancing aunties; however, Noah managed to have heaps of fun on the dance floor. He won't have noticed any difference between the parties, he just loved all the attention and the presents – but we felt really happy that everyone was catered for, and it was such a happy time.

In this first year, every day was new. We watched Noah learn to roll over, and smile, and recognise our voices. He held up his arms for us to pick him up and he'd get so excited when Money came home from work. His first word was 'dada', when he was around six months old, and I was dying for him to then say 'mama', but it took quite a while for him to get that one. He became the most social little butterfly, like his dad, and he still loves being around people and interacting and exploring the world. I could not be more proud. As someone who has been shy her entire life, it makes me so happy to see that my son has no fear but just dives head-first into every situation. I love that about him. He has these very important people in his life within the two families; I'm sure they almost love him more than we do, and Noah loves them back. He goes crazy when he can hear them arriving at our place or coming up the stairs. And he knows how to hold the phone and chatter to them in baby language on FaceTime if they're not with us in person.

We decided to invent our own ritual. On the date of Noah's birth, so, the twentieth of every month for the whole of his first year, we had a celebration at home with our sets of parents. There was a cake with candles, and a dinner together, sometimes curries and favourite Indian foods, other times just pizzas or takeaways, but it was about everyone knowing it was booked in and we'd all be there. It was such a nice way to get the family around the table, and to be able to acknowledge our little boy and all that he gives us.

We went on a holiday to Mount Manganui for the first time with Noah when he was about ten months old. It was so good to get away from Auckland and to spend that time, just the three of us. It's a beautiful part of the country and we climbed to the top of the mount and explored the area. We managed to vlog heaps of it, so it's very cool to have this holiday on record and Noah can watch it when he is older. And on that holiday, Noah took his first steps, and by the end of it, he was a pro at walking. Such a clever boy.

He surprises us and makes us laugh and brings us so much joy. Now that he is a toddler, he's able to show us more what he wants and who he is, and each day just seems to get better. We feel so incredibly grateful to be able to live the way we do, both getting to spend all this time with our son. It is a dream come true! We've worked hard to keep to a routine during the day so we know what we're doing. Sometimes we manage it. We've tried and failed and tried again to get him to sleep through the night, so that we can too, and his bedtime has its routine to settle him down for the night. In terms of day-to-day life, usually it's wake up, feed and change him, then we spend the morning hanging out and playing with him. Most days, Noah visits his *Dadi-ji* (Money's mum) and will play there while we go to the gym. Then we'll take him home for his nap – which is also when we'll shower and get ready for recording a video. Most afternoons, we all hang out together, I will cook dinner and we eat as a family, and often we will have more family over for dinner to join us. Once Noah goes to bed, we edit the videos, upload them, then finally it's time for Money and me to relax and spend some time together – or sleep! On the days we are not recording, we usually take Noah to one of the indoor playgrounds or he has playdates with his little friends – it's about making his day as fun as possible, which makes our day fun. Our main goal is always ensuring he is happy and well cared for. And because we have such amazing support around us, if we are recording a video that will take up too much time, Noah will go to one of his grandmothers, who are always dying to have him.

Raising Noah has been a lot different than we expected – but I'm not really sure what we expected. Maybe parenthood never meets expectations, but it still is better than I could have imagined. You can never prepare for it, and it's learning on the job every day, but it has literally been the most rewarding and incredible thing we have ever done in our lives. Noah could not be more adored! I could not have asked for more, he's everything we've ever wanted – and now we are lucky enough to have another one on the way, and we get to do it all over again, and we already know Noah will be an awesome big brother.

CHAPTER SEVENTEEN

Cooking with Mummy-ji

MONEY

One of the many things that I love about Abbey is how important family is to her; she's definitely the one who brought me back to my family. She is always encouraging us to get together with them and she creates occasions when we can share a meal and hang out. Compared to the beginning of our relationship, when my parents wouldn't even hear her name mentioned, I still can't believe how far we have come. Mum and Dad love Abbey. I will always remember, around the time of the weddings, when Abbey's father had said he wasn't going to be at our wedding and Abbey was really upset, my dad said to her: 'I'm also your dad, Abbey. Don't worry, you have a father here in me.' We both loved that moment so much. And I think this is what our followers online really like and why they keep asking us to put more videos up, because they love our family relationship and how well we get on. They like seeing Abbey with my brother or sitting around the table with my parents and laughing and chatting. It is so fun showing them our lives like this and including them.

Even though Abbey's family are quite camera-shy and don't like being shown online very much, I have fitted in really well with them, too. I have been able to chill out with Abbey's mum since Abbey and I were first dating, and her house became a refuge for me from all the drama going on at mine. I'll always be grateful for how she accepted me as Abbey's partner and was there for us. Abbey says I go above and beyond for her mum. I'm not sure, but I do love fixing things and getting her place in order (because I like things to be tidy), and Abbey's mum is fine with whatever I want to do. I've been known to rearrange her whole living room when I think there's a better way it can work and shift the furniture to flow better. I'll install or fix the dishwasher and do other things around the house.

One time, I planned the biggest surprise of all, which was so exciting and I couldn't wait to show Abbey's mum. She often talked to me about the best car she'd ever had, years ago, which was a Mercedes A180. She said it was a silver hatchback and that she'd never found a car as good as that one. When the car she had now needed to be repaired quite extensively, I had another idea. I didn't even tell Abbey, but I found a Mercedes A180 on TradeMe – the exact model and colour as her mum's old one. I put it in our garage and called Abbey's mum to come and see something. For the first few minutes as she stood looking at it, she was excited for me that I had bought a car and how funny that it was the same one she'd had. It took ages for it to dawn on her what I'd done. I had to keep telling her, 'It's for you. I got it for you.' It was a really fun surprise.

Abbey and I cannot believe how close her relationship with my mum has become but, for me as the son who brought Abbey into our family, it makes my heart burst with pride to see how well they get on and how amazing the cooking is they do together – and I get to taste it all: double bonus. Our online followers cannot get enough of the two of them. We have to keep thinking of more ideas and food for them to cook so our viewers can watch Mum and Abbey together. There are always thousands and thousands of comments. When they cooked *aloo paratha* (flatbread stuffed with spiced potatoes), so many people were really moved by the video. They loved Abbey understanding what my mum was saying in Punjabi, and her picking up the traditional techniques and working alongside my mum. It matters so much for people to see their closeness and that this sort of interracial relationship can actually work. We love reading all the comments, like these:

- *This family is sharing a loving relationship. God bless you all.*
- *I love watching you and your family cooking together and just enjoying each other. Thanks for your efforts in producing such great content.*
- *Beautiful and lovely family, I was looking for a aloo paratha recipe and I got so much more, love your chemistry and humour.*
- *Omg the mother in law and wife's relationship is so cute and wholesome; Beautiful family! Love the mother and daughter relationship. That's a good mother who raised a good son and I love the way she treats her daughter in law like her actual daughter. so many people could learn from you guys :)*
- *Just love the love with which the food is being made. Mom in law is teaching so lovingly along with Punjabi tips. Even I learned a few Punjabi words today. This is one lovely paratha.*

No wonder it makes us feel good and want to keep producing the videos when we receive feedback like this. It still amazes me and makes me laugh as I film these clips that this is actually my mum in front of the camera. She just loves being the star, now. She would be on the videos the whole time if she could – she's often the one saying, 'Get your camera out, Money!' And my dad and brother are okay with being filmed as well. Abbey's family, not so much. Our families feel differently about being involved in our posts, which gives some people the wrong idea and they think we must spend all our time with only my family, which is not the case. Abbey's mum has some really stressful, busy times as a midwife, and although she is proud of us and loves what we are doing, she needs to be able to just do her job and not be recognised or have to talk about us when someone is going through a difficult labour, for example. As for my extended family, now I get my aunties coming up and telling me to make sure I give them warning if they're going to be on, because they want to look nice. They always hear straightaway from family members overseas, saying, 'Oh, I could see you on that video.' It's no longer just Abbey and me in The Modern Singhs!

ABBEY

Coming into this huge extended family of Money's was like nothing I had experienced before. If his family has an event to celebrate, they don't need to invite outsiders, they just ask the immediate family and they already have a massive party on their hands. And there are so many occasions and festivals. The most well known one we celebrate every year is *Diwali*, in November. We prepare for it by cleaning the entire home (like a big spring-clean). It's a festival of new beginnings and of light fighting out darkness, so the whole inside and outside of the house is lit up with lights and candles are everywhere and it is really beautiful. We go around the relatives' houses and our own, saying a quick prayer in each and having some nuts or sweets, which symbolises us giving our blessing to that house and family. Usually, by the last house, we will have a big dinner that has been prepared by everyone and there are fireworks too. In Auckland city, they hold a *Diwali* festival and that is so much fun! We have gone for the past few years – they have food, performances and Indian clothing and jewellery to buy. It's brilliant.

One festival that we loved this year is called *Lohri*. It's usually held on the longest night of the year to recognise that sunny days are arriving. Everyone in the community wishes each other 'happy *Lohri*' and they light a bonfire. A *Lohri* can also be held for newlyweds and parents with a newborn baby, so naturally Money's parents wanted us to have one. Ours was held at a local Indian restaurant that had lots of space out the back for us all. It was such an amazing atmosphere, with everyone singing and dancing around the bonfire. The idea is to throw foods like *gajak* (a sweet made with sesame seeds), popcorn, puffed rice and peanuts into the flames, as 'tributes' to the gods in exchange for blessings. It was a really good excuse to get together and have a party. We recorded it all for YouTube so everyone following us online could be a part of it.

Back in the early days, Money and I were comfortable hanging out at each other's houses, but it was a big deal bringing our families together for the first time. It was at Money's parents' house and we were there for dinner. They all got on well, but there was the obvious language barrier. Pam would say something to start the conversation and my mum would reply in her thick Scottish accent. Pam couldn't understand a word she was saying and didn't know how to respond so she'd just nod her head and smile and change the conversation. These days my mum knows to only use short words and give brief answers. That is as much as they can communicate, although it is gradually improving. Money's dad is self-conscious about his English and avoids speaking it – until he has had a few drinks, then he speaks really well and you can have a good conversation with him. He is basically a shy person, especially around new people.

He always worries that he will say the wrong thing, and alcohol is his confidence booster. I remember when I met the family for the first time, on Ash's birthday, Money's dad had already had a few drinks and started speaking to me in English. Money and I were shocked: *What? He can speak so much English?* He says he won't speak it much because he has a finite number of words and doesn't want to use them up.

Money's dad is very thoughtful. One day, he asked me what my mother's favourite wine was and wrote down the name, then he bought a bottle before the two families were having dinner. He still has that label in his wallet and he will go and buy that wine whenever we're about to meet up.

My stepdad, Mike, loves Pam's (*Mummy-ji's*) cooking. He is obsessed with her curries. Because she knows this, one time she made four curries for one dinner. That was such a bonding occasion. Mike has been in our lives for a few years now. He has two younger children. He married Mum in 2019. They began dating after Money and I got together, and we could soon tell it was serious. I don't think Mum was prepared to have another relationship – until she met Mike. The day I moved out, he moved in. It is so nice to see her in a happy relationship with so much love in her life. When the two families are together, these are some of my happiest times. Our mums will be in one corner talking about Noah and the two dads will be chatting about anything at all.

Then both couples gradually start talking to each other and swapping stories about my childhood and Money's childhood. It makes me feel very grateful for what we have and what we've been through to get to this point.

Money's mum and I have been through so much. The arguments and fights between Money and his parents in the early days made me nervous to even meet her because I felt guilty, but I also wanted to so she could see how much I cared about her son. Then there was the horrible time after Noah was born, and because I was feeling so low, I didn't have the same energy or drive to sort things out with her. I just needed space and we had to give our relationship time to repair. But time always heals, and it did with us. I went to her place almost every day with Noah. We still spend hours together. We chat very easily and love sharing Noah time. She tells me stories about Money's childhood and what her own upbringing was like, about her staying at the in-law's home in Bowani and how different it was coming to New Zealand. Gradually, we just got back to where we were before Noah – only so much closer.

Money's mum has been my biggest supporter for learning the Punjabi culture and way of living, and it was cooking together that was the breakthrough. Money says it was always her dream to have a daughter or a daughter-in-law she could share her knowledge with, and I remember early on, when we were still just dating, I asked her how she had made the *roti* and the curry she had just cooked for us. She was so excited that day.

'Come over and I will show you everything,' she said. 'I would love you to learn to cook these foods.'

I am not the best of cooks. I do love baking and I used to always enjoy cooking with my granny, but this was on a completely different scale. I had never eaten Indian food before I tasted Pam's dishes, and I used to hate anything that had spices in it. I was hopeless at trying new foods and would refuse to eat a dish if I thought it might be too hot. To think that then I married an Indian guy and now I love the spicy curries – although at the beginning, she kept them very mild, slowly increasing the amount of chilli as my tolerance grew. Each time we cooked together, I was frantically taking down everything she said on notes on my phone but she cooked and talked so fast! She wasn't used to having to do things slowly or explaining herself so I was just trying my best to keep up. It was frantic and I didn't want to miss any of it. She would say most of the ingredients in Punjabi or quickly explain it in English once and then in Punjabi after that. Sometimes, I'd have to write down the Punjabi word and then ask Money when I got home, 'What is *adarak* again?' and he would remind me it was ginger, and I would correct it in my notes. It turned out to be such a great way for me to learn the language. When I'd get back home I'd try them out – but not until a few days later because she'd give us containers full of the food we'd just cooked. I have to say every recipe Money's mum has given me has been delicious and has always turned out well, so it makes me happy that I can share them with others to try and they can taste just how good her food is.

The kitchen is *Mummy-ji*'s happy place and it has become mine, too. I get so excited when I have mastered a dish. I first learnt how to cook *daal*, and we put that up on a video. Then she showed me how to make *saag*, and we videoed that. But soon we realised that we may as well have her there too, seeing we were already cooking together anyway. Money's mum just loves being part of our YouTube vlogs. And we found that our followers went crazy for it. It was so unique to see the two of us in the kitchen, side by side, me being taught how to make these wonderful Indian meals. One time, my mum was involved, too, the three of us making *roti*, one rolling the dough into balls, one flattening it and the other cooking and turning it over the heat. It was a very cool occasion in the kitchen.

The other way we bond is through the clothes she makes for me. Money's mum is an amazing seamstress; she can just see something in her head, she'll go and find fabric, often from a second-hand store, and sew it up, every stitch of it.

I can't even think how many times people have asked me online where did I get my Punjabi suit, and I love saying my mother-in-law made it for me. People ask her all the time now whether she could make them some clothes as well, even family members ask, but she says she doesn't want to make them for anyone but me and Ash's future wife, as we are her daughters. I have always felt so touched by this, and I just love wearing the clothes she makes me. I have so many beautiful outfits. She used to always want a daughter so she could dress her up and put her in the suits she'd made, and now she says she has one. And she's really skilled and is into designing clothes. In fact, she made and stitched her own wedding outfit – the *chunni*, *salwar* (loose, pleated trousers) and suit – which is incredible. Money's dad also sews and he made Money and Noah matching *kurta* (traditional Punjabi clothing for men, usually a very long shirt), and they look very handsome in them. Then when his mum was in India the last time, she brought back suits for me that match their *kurta*. Just another really thoughtful gesture. We are so fortunate with our two families and what they do for us, we can't believe it sometimes.

CHAPTER EIGHTEEN

YouTube Famous

MONEY

Even seeing that title 'YouTube Famous' still doesn't seem real – and it makes us straightaway want to explain ourselves in case people get the wrong idea about who we are. But, social media is what people question us about the most, so we'll try and explain how it works and how we manage our channels. And explain what we get out of it, what drives us, why our followers matter so much, and what the future holds.

For us and our family, the world of social media was a complete unknown, even the bank and our accountant didn't get it when we first went to them. So, in simple terms, the way someone makes money on YouTube is from the advertisements played before, during and after their video. That is pretty much it. Those ads pay the people who have put up the video, and they pay YouTube, and Google, which owns YouTube. Once we have given YouTube permission to put the ads on, they do the rest; payment is calculated automatically. But we only get paid if people watch the whole advertisement. If they choose the skip-after-five-seconds option, we don't make any money, nor is it based on how many views the video has. Obviously, the more people, the greater the number who will potentially watch the ads, and because it has the power of Google behind it, YouTube tailors the ads to each viewer. It knows what else you have been watching on YouTube and finds things you might be interested in. Someone in Auckland might see a different ad than someone in Wellington, and people watching our videos in India will definitely be getting different ads from people in New Zealand. Our only say in this is selecting how many ads we allow. For The Modern Singhs, we choose to have one at the start, two in the middle and one at the end, then YouTube works out what these will be and places them. We want to keep the number of advertisements to a minimum because we know how annoying it is when you are watching something and an ads pops up.

There are ways of making extra money from your online presence: you can place more ads around the videos, accept sponsorships and do product mentions. We do some of the last two, but not very often and certainly not as much as is being offered to us. About once a month, we might feature in an ad ourselves, but we don't go out looking for deals. Doing just a few ads lets our viewers know there must be something worthwhile about that company and product for us to accept.

People who upload videos ask for 'likes' and subscribers, as this helps increase their online presence. We made a joke about it early on, which has become our 'thing', where Abbey starts saying, 'If you like this video, please remember to like …' and as soon as she says 'like', I say 'We aren't that couple', and it blurs out her request and it is done. We don't suggest viewers follow us. If they enjoy it and want to see more clips, that's great, we love that, but we won't explicitly ask. It just makes us feel better about this world we're in that can be quite false, when we can stay light-hearted and authentic.

We started getting popular on YouTube and that was when we needed to take it more seriously. The numbers were pretty crazy, and still are, actually. I remember for the first few videos we were getting around maybe 10,000–15,000 views in a day, and we were like, *Whaaat?* And then when Abbey found out she was pregnant, we were getting 10,000 views in an hour, which just seemed insane, and then within 24 hours of our videos being live after Noah's birth, we had over a million views. These numbers still fluctuate, often, but we do feel very blessed that so many people want to tune in and see what we are up to. You have no idea how many times we look at each other and think, why us? Why are people even interested? But we had to work out what to do. We certainly didn't have a wedding or a birth video to upload every week – thank goodness – so we chose to do our own thing, recording ourselves doing everyday things, showing our family and what matters to us, and we hoped people would like it.

Social media feels like a hungry dog, sometimes. Once we were on YouTube, we worked out that a good balance would be to upload a new video clip every second day. Then we needed an Instagram page because people wanted more; then it was a Facebook page. TikTok came along and we had to get onto that as you have to stay with the trends or you can become irrelevant really quickly. TikTok was increasing in popularity so fast, and it just requires 15 seconds of material at a time, like a skit, a dance or maybe lip-synching to a Punjabi song. This grew the fastest and led to a big increase in our Instagram numbers. But then TikTok got banned in India, which at first was a worry, because this is where most of our followers are, but the short Instagram reels work the same way as TikTok, so we've maintained those viewers after all.

I honestly don't think we're that great with our social media. We never saw YouTube as a career until quite recently when it grew too big for us to manage as a side interest, so in lots of ways we're learning as we go. Most of our videos aren't planned and seeing us just laughing and joking around is very typical. We don't use scripts, but we do write down ideas in a notebook as they come to us.

Some ideas for clips work better than others, but we can never tell when a video is going to soar or crash and burn. Once, we were doing a cooking video and everything was funny and we were being silly and I called Abbey 'crazy' in Punjabi. 'It means "beautiful",' I added.

'I know exactly what it means!' Abbey said. We laughed so hard and we just couldn't stop. People loved seeing us so natural like this and there were so many views for that one. It actually went viral and was posted on numerous accounts and news pages – it was pretty crazy. I think that's when people really started to look us up on TikTok and Instagram and get to know our story.

If we are doing a cooking vlog, we need to do some preparation to make sure we have all the ingredients and equipment we need, but usually, we just go for it and start filming. Our viewers know that Abbey isn't wearing Punjabi suits the whole time or spending every day making *roti* in the kitchen. Like any job, we have work hours, where we get prepared and dress up if that is what is needed that day, and start the recording. So much of it is trial and error, and we are learning all the time. That is the fun of it, but it is also quite stressful. We have to be aware of what our viewers want or ask for, without actually knowing whether it will work, although I think we're getting better at knowing which things are likely to be popular.

With a video clip showing Abbey and my mum cooking an Indian curry, the views will reach a million very quickly. People tell us they follow the recipes and message us how good they are. One day, I was cooking in Mum's kitchen and I randomly made up this phrase: 'It smells so good, it looks so good and it tastes so good.' Now we have to use that in every cooking video because if I don't say it, people write in and remind me, or they think there must be something wrong with the food. As well, people always like watching us try different snacks from various countries. It's about seeing somebody's reaction, I think, especially a food that the viewer knows already; but a few times we've videoed Abbey trying Punjabi snacks, and now that Noah is getting older, we give him some to try and film his reactions. These get a huge response online.

We are not really 'social media people' as such. We know how many likes or shares we get for our posts, but we don't constantly check the numbers to make ourselves feel good. We upload regularly onto YouTube because it's where we feel most loyal to our followers, and what we enjoy doing the most. We only put reels on TikTok when we feel like it. We haven't done any research about what works or doesn't work online. We like to sometimes check out other people who are doing similar clips to us, but not often. I basically learnt how to make YouTube videos by watching YouTube videos. It's where I found out about the vlog cameras we use. I have a Canon EOS M50 that I really like. I used to have a Powershot G7X but it had no microphone input and it required a handheld tripod, which is too fiddly and awkward to use when we're out and about. With this bigger camera, we feel more confident filming outside and in public places as it looks more professional. As with any job, having the right tools and equipment sets you up well, but we still keep it as simple as possible. We don't use a drone for extra shots, for example. If you have a drone, then you have to think up extra things to do to make use of it – it's not a natural process. We're not an adventure channel, we're a family channel.

There's so much we didn't know about online protocols and behaviour before we began this career. One time in the early days, we were asked to take down a cooking video we had made. We were issued a copyright strike from another vlogger who does cooking clips, claiming we'd violated their copyright. Our video showed Abbey making *aloo paratha* and it was so popular it got a million views in two days. But when we'd filmed it, I'd forgotten to take an actual photo of our *roti* to use for the thumbnail, so I went on Google and copied and pasted a picture of *roti* and used this instead. It was so small, and it didn't even feature in our actual video, and I didn't think about it again, but the person who took the original photo made a complaint, which was enough for us to have to take our video down. When we were issued the strike, we immediately emailed to apologise, and we asked them to accept this and withdraw it. We also offered a shout-out to them as a way of people finding out more about their site, but they never replied and there was nothing we could do. This is the way of the online domain. We just have to be really careful and never cross those lines, even unintentionally. Because we now understand how much harm a strike can do, we try to be generous when it happens to us. When people use our content, we always issue a strike first to show we're not happy, and if they contact us and apologise, we withdraw it and ask them not to use our content without our permission. After we got that strike against us, I deleted every thumbnail on every video we'd ever done and my brother taught me how to make thumbnails so this mistake wouldn't happen again.

One consideration for us is which language to use and how we choose to manage this. It is such a huge topic of conversation and comment online. We speak English in most of our videos because it means more people can watch them, and many of our viewers who don't speak English as their first language have told us that watching the videos has helped them in their attempts to learn English. We are different to other Indian vloggers in that we choose to communicate more in English, but partly this is because Abbey can't speak much Punjabi – although that is improving every day and now she corrects me with words. If Punjabi is being spoken, we try to add subtitles or I will say it first in Punjabi and then translate it, so that all our viewers can understand. We aim to be about 50:50 Punjabi- and English-speaking, to be as inclusive as we can.

ABBEY

The only content we post online is family content. When thinking of what to record, we always keep in mind that we want both the youngest and the oldest members of a family to be able to watch us. This is so important because family is our world. It's why our vibe is this friendly, fun, family dynamic, because that's how we live, and we hope it makes others aim to keep family close. We want to show how beautiful family relationships can be when you put in the effort, even if there are hard times. We like to make people smile and laugh, and to feel as happy as we feel. We love sharing the cooking videos. It's the way Money's mum and I have bonded, and, hopefully, others can try this in their interracial households. Judging from the thousands of comments after any of these videos, we know it makes people give it a go, or they talk about how they wish that they had done this, or they share the clip with others who need it. I love seeing the comments and the photos they send of their food. Being able to cook a meal and put it on the table and have everyone bond over food and spend time together – nothing is more special to us. It's our happy place.

We have the best time filming and sharing on The Modern Singhs channel. What fills us with pride is that our relationship has become something others love to watch and want for themselves; they tell us it gives them hope. In our local Sikh community, we're told all the time how much they love us and they love what we've done to show the world the special nature of the Punjabi culture. They see that our modern ways can cross over racial divides. Sharing our recipes, dances, cultural events and family is our way to connect to people. When we started, we didn't see many other interracial couples posting online. It's definitely a big trend now and we're really happy about that.

There is a huge amount of responsibility that comes with what we're doing. What started out as a way for people to see our wedding videos has turned into something we can't even comprehend. And we can't turn our backs on it, because we're receiving love back, hundreds of comments a day, from people who are now part of our lives. That sounds crazy, when this is all being done online, but we can see the statistics, and there are viewers who have posted comments to us more than 800 times. That's a really big commitment from them, and we owe it to those followers to appreciate and respect this.

Just the other day, I was reading a beautiful comment from someone saying she is in hospital and suffering from mental-health issues and that waiting for another video clip from us was what was keeping her going and that it is the only thing that is making her happy at the moment. How can we look away from this or not take it seriously? It makes us feel humble.

We don't know how big is the impact that The Modern Singhs has out there, yet we try hard to engage with as many followers as possible. We genuinely love them; there's this huge family now that we are part of. It is overwhelming but it is also beautiful and we cannot get over the love and support we receive every day.

Of course, it goes without saying that there is a negative side to social media. Everyone knows there are people out there who spend their time pulling others down. Some of the feedback we receive and how nasty the trolls can be, hiding behind their screen to criticise and say terrible things, is unbelievable and very hard to deal with or get over. We are so grateful we have each other and we have learnt over time to not dwell on the negatives. If the whole of social media were wiped out overnight, we would still have all the things that are important – each other, our children, our families, our friends. We are bigger than the hurt that haters try to inflict, and the people close to us help us deal with it.

But we did have to work out ways around negative feedback in those early days. Human nature shows that if you receive 100 comments and only one is negative, that's the one you pay attention to. The hardest negative comments to read were when I was pregnant. I was so emotional anyway but horrible comments really hurt. They made me not want to leave the house or post any more. I knew I was supposed to ignore them and not react but that's not easy. In hindsight, we regret replying to negative people and wish we had focused more on the positive comments instead of wasting our time with the negative ones, but a few times when we received something really abusive, we replied. It's incredible – often, as soon as you reply, people's attitudes change. '*Oh I'm so sorry. We love you guys, I didn't mean it like that. I didn't know you would actually see what I said.*' Really? So why say it at all.

There was one especially horrible one that I can't even repeat but it stayed with me. I couldn't stop thinking about it. I blocked the person then did an Instagram post saying anyone who feels like that about me should just unfollow me. I was so broken, and I was posting in anger and tears. Hundreds of messages of love and appreciation came flooding in and it gave me some perspective. I realised it was wrong to get mad about one person and certainly it wasn't worth focusing on them. It is so good we have each other, as well. Money came up with the plan of ignoring all negative comments and only replying to the positive ones. Then we end up feeling great and uplifted by all the love. The thing haters hate the most is being ignored. If you react, they will just send more hate. So it is very satisfying to ignore them. I think those who feel the need to hurt others on social media must forget there is a real person at the other end receiving them. We know the people saying hateful things are miserable in themselves, but knowing that doesn't really make you feel better at the time. We've just got so much better at only concentrating on all the good that is coming out of this, and we truly love our supporters so much and they are what keep us putting up our videos and thinking of ways to engage with them.

There's a kind of comment that isn't quite racist, but is sort of. I love doing *bhangra* dances, but when I did them on TikTok, people would send mean messages: '*You are just trying to be Punjabi. You will never be as good as us. Why are you trying to spoil our culture*?' Fair enough – those girls will always be better at *bhangra*; it is their culture, not mine, and I have never assumed I am terribly good at this dance, but it makes me feel amazing and there is such an important difference between appreciating another culture and showing you love it, as opposed to trying to take it over as your own. That I would never do. But just like other hateful comments, those who try to put me down for dancing should think instead about supporting someone for showing respect to it enough that they want to learn it.

If a person's mental health is already fragile, comments on social media can send them over the edge, especially for some reason when on TikTok, where people make a fake account, invent a name and go for gold being spiteful. New Zealand creators get a lot of hate on TikTok. You have to be mentally strong to withstand it, and if comments break you and you don't have someone to support you, you shouldn't upload stuff onto that platform. We both still have to work at dealing with the negativity and we look out for each other, and we've learnt to shrug and say, 'Well, this is me; this is who I am.' When I was pregnant I purposely did our vlogs wearing no makeup because we were vlogging about our day-to-day life. I was tired all the time. I wanted to let people know that if you're pregnant you don't have to look glamorous, so I tied my hair back and showed them what a real pregnancy looked like and people respected it. Most people. There were ones who wrote '*You look so fat, it's disgusting.*' They got blocked. It's their loss. We had so many women writing in thanking us for me showing them my natural self, it was amazing.

We can't reply to every comment because we get so many, but I like to reply to girls who send messages along the lines of '*I wish I looked different*'. I hate to think they don't like the way they look and they think they need to change something. I remind them that so many people they admire online have filters and full makeup and a hair stylist to ensure they look the way they do. It is why I make a point of showing my real face on YouTube. I had to learn this. I wasn't always this way. When we started, I was insecure and scared of hate comments. Before we recorded anything, I got full makeup and fake eyelashes and tried so hard and then I understood that I didn't need to. Now I just want to look how I am. I think this is so important, especially when we have an audience of teenage girls.

Not everything about our feedback is bad, of course. I wish we could reply to all the beautiful comments we get. We have a process we follow when we upload a new video. We stay online and reply to comments for half an hour, then we put our phones down and switch off and do other things.

When we started our YouTube career, we would only get ten or twenty comments and it was easy to deal with them. We would reply to them all and it was a great way to build trust with our followers. We still try to keep up with our followers as best we can; we do lives, Q&As on Instagram, we interact a lot with our fan pages, and we reply to many comments. Our subscribers mean so much to us and we always want to stay connected to them.

Sometimes, we get caught up in controversies that don't even matter, like when I dyed my hair. I have naturally blonde hair, which I wear long, as most people know from the videos. But in April 2021, I dyed it brown. Oh my goodness. We got *thousands* of messages. Many of them were really positive and we got a lot of love, but others were upset and were so critical and disapproving. There was also some hate, with people saying I was trying to become Punjabi and that Money was making me lose my sense of self. Of course, we knew this wasn't true, but it kind of alarmed us and reminded us that just because we have followers on social media, it doesn't necessarily mean they are all there to support us. I can't imagine telling someone I didn't like their hair. I can imagine not liking it, but why would I think they would care about my opinion to the point that I would write in and say something? '*Just letting you know, your colour is really bad and you should go back to blonde*'; '*Your husband is forcing you to be*

Indian.' It was extraordinary. And made no sense. As if going dark automatically means I'm changing my whole culture. I enjoyed having dark hair for a while. It was just something spontaneous I did. We had no idea it would create such a storm, but it's made us even more determined to do everything we want without first anticipating what the feedback might be. We won't give others that sort of control over us.

After we had been on YouTube for a long time, we decided to film a video where we go right back to the beginning, telling people about our struggles to get Money's parents to accept our relationship. We got so much feedback; a lot of people wanted to talk about their own experiences. So many related to it because they had been through something similar, some with a happy ending; some that ended up in arranged marriages. And it wasn't only a match with an Indian person; there were people from different cultures contacting us from all around the world where religion and cultural beliefs restrict their attempts to have a relationship, despite their differences. It's these sorts of discussions that make us so pleased we have made our lives available for others to view, because we have given so many people hope and we are an example they can follow.

In terms of our future, we want to preserve the YouTube channel for as long as we can – it's something we truly love to do. We keep talking about how much we'd love to open a restaurant one day, as a family-run business. We have said so often how we enjoy cooking and putting a meal on the table for the family, so this would be a real dream. Money has a cousin who is a chef in New Zealand, and for our customers, we have enough family to provide for! It would be super cool, but at this stage that's just a dream. We also potentially would like to get into music, as we made an intro song for YouTube that I sang and people loved it, and it's something I really enjoy doing so maybe that would be fun to pursue and see where it takes me. It's something that I could vlog along the way and maybe even help to grow our channel, but again, who knows. We have been working on creating a full song with a producer friend, Lepani, who wrote the introduction song, so we can't wait to see where that takes us. Although, if none of these things ended up working out, I think Money would really enjoy going back to tech solutions work, and I would continue my studies to get my masters in Psychology and try to work on a more professional career, which I plan on doing down the track when our social media life isn't as prominent or busy.

In terms of our personal lives, we just always want to be this close to each other and to our family, and concentrate on raising our children.

EPILOGUE

The Last Word

ABBEY & MONEY

Our two mothers often have the last word, so it should be no surprise our book is going to end with them. They're our heroes. They brought us into the world, they made the decision to leave their home countries and emigrate to New Zealand and they taught us their values, ensuring we always try to be strong, loving and caring people. Both our mothers are so important to us, and now to Noah – and soon, hopefully, to mini Singh.

We asked them how they feel watching us grow up as New Zealanders and start our own family here. To have come from two different countries and now choose

Auckland as where we want our home has made us wonder what it's been like for them. Pam, *Mummy-ji*, told us she feels really proud that her son and grandchildren's futures are bright and promising here, with the opportunities this country offers. She said that this is a place where we can fulfil all our wishes and goals. New Zealand feels like home to her and Dad now, so even though India will always take up a huge part of our family's heart, they are so pleased to be living here. They have their *Gurdwara*, their community, their family all around them, they have us down the road, they have Abbey's family now, and they feel happy.

Theresa told us she's really proud of Abbey, and that she's been able to achieve everything she's wanted since making the decision to move to New Zealand. She knows there were tough times, but, sometimes, it doesn't feel like that long ago since they moved here. She said at first she was surprised Abbey wanted to start a family so young, 'but it was quickly obvious the time was right for you both because everything has just fallen into place. Once I'd met Money, I could see why Abbey would never go anywhere else or be with anyone else.'

Our relationship is very special to us and it's built on love and trust and a lot of hard work and honesty. Pam says she loves the bond we have. 'You guys have a very good understanding of each other. You are giving Noah a good future and you are raising him very nicely, and this is because you treat each other equally, that one of you is not more or less than the other.' This is so good for us to hear from her, especially considering the difficult road we all started on. Theresa says, 'From when I first saw you two together, I knew it was meant to be, and that you were happy. I think when you've found that somebody, you just know, and it shows. I could see you two together for the rest of your lives.'

We've been reflecting as well on what love means. Coming from an arranged marriage herself and initially fighting so hard for our relationship *not* to happen, Pam says that what she used to think previously, she now knows was wrong. 'I was too narrow-minded. I'm so glad I changed my mind about the whole situation and you two ended up getting married. I thank Waheguru Ji every day that I made that decision.' She says, 'Honestly, I see you like Romeo and Juliet; everyone should have this kind of love. You have more understanding than love. You can really only love someone if you understand them. Yours is like loving the inside of someone, not just the outside – you love each other to your souls. People always want this kind of love you share.'

For Theresa, another reason why she thinks our love works is because in some ways we are opposites and in some ways very similar. 'I would have thought there were things that could have broken you, such as what a neat freak Money is and how untidy Abbey … *was*. I remember taking a photo of her bedroom and threatening to show it to Money – and now she's a neat freak as well. But you know love when you see it. And Money just fitted into the family right away.' Abbey's mum was too shy to make a speech on our European wedding day, so she asked the band to sing a song that she said described exactly how she felt about our relationship. It's called 'I Loved Her First' and is such a beautiful idea about the love of a parent, then witnessing someone else loving your child. It's like a parent passing on the responsibility of love and care, from the family you were born into, to the family that you will create for yourself. One of the lyrics Abbey's mum identifies with says that it's almost like she knew more than Abbey did at the time: that from seeing us together, she knew the moment had come.

We don't know if we believe in fate or destiny, but from our very first date there was something inexplicably wonderful between us. Whether it's Romeo and Juliet, or whether this kind of magic happens every day somewhere in the world, mums are always right. Our love was only a matter of time.

Acknowledgements

We would love to say the biggest thank you to our families, for always showing us so much support in our lives. It is because of you that any of this is able to happen, and your support and love mean the world to us.

We would also love to thank all our subscribers and anyone who has decided to read our story. Your support truly touches our hearts, and we could not be more grateful for this opportunity that we live every day. We hope that by reading this book you are able to see just how much each one of you means to us and how thankful we are.

We would also like to say a big thank you to Paul Little and Judith Watson, for helping us to tell our story. Without you this book would not have been possible, and we are so grateful to you both.

And lastly, we would like to thank our children, for making us who we are today and for inspiring us, every single day, to do better and be better people. We love you so much.